PLACES IN SYRIA

A Pocket Grand Tour

PLACES IN SYRIA

A Pocket Grand Tour

FRANCIS RUSSELL

F

FRANCES LINCOLN LIMITED
PUBLISHERS

CONTENTS

For Drue Heinz
most perceptive and
generous of friends

Frances Lincoln Limited
4 Torriano Mews
Torriano Avenue
London NW5 2RZ
www.franceslincoln.com

Places in Syria

First Frances Lincoln edition 2011

A catalogue record for this book is available from the British Library.

ISBN: 978-0-7112-3166-5

Printed and bound in China

9 8 7 6 5 4 3 2 1

Page 2 **The mosaic from Umm Galal, sixth century** AD
Opposite **The temple in Dumeir: detail.**

INTRODUCTION

In simple trust like theirs who heard
Beside the Syrian sea
The gracious calling of their Lord

How many of us brought up on that most compelling of anthologies, the hymnal, learn first of Syria through the words of the American poet James Greenleaf Whittier, who, of course, was referring to the Lake of Galilee, now largely outside the modern state of Syria, which encompasses only part of the greater Syria of the past.

Syria stretches from the Mediterranean in the west to the Jezira – the land between the Tigris and the Euphrates – in the east. While the narrow coastal plain and the mountain ranges that encroach upon this, except to the west of Homs, are well watered, the land to the east is heavily dependent on three major rivers: the Euphrates, flowing south-east from the Turkish border; the Orontes – rising in the Bekaa valley, now in the Lebanon – which curls majestically though Hama and then cuts through to a great enclosed valley, the Ghab, to cross the Turkish frontier and reach the sea below Antioch; and the Barada, which drains from the Anti-Lebanon, watering Damascus and its oasis, before dying in the desert. Some distance north of Damascus a range of hills extends north-eastwards and catches enough rain to supply the oasis of Palmyra. South of Damascus, beyond the rich volcanic earth of the Ledja, is the Jebel al-Arab, or Jebel Druze, where enough rain falls to ensure fertility. But great tracts of the country have historically remained desert or semi-

Palmyra: the Temple of Bel.

desert, challenging successive inhabitants to harness the limited water resources at their disposal.

Geographical factors partly explain why Syria has for millennia been close to the very pulse of the evolution of what we term civilization. At Ugarit, Ebla and Mari archaeologists have unearthed some of the most sophisticated of early civilizations. The Phoenician past remains a palpable presence at Arwad and Amrit; Damascus is still bound by the plan of the original Seleucid city; while Roman rule is as evident at Apamea and Isriya, Bosra and Shahba, as Palmyrene economic power is at Palmyra itself. The 'dead cities' of the limestone hills west and south of Aleppo, the pilgrimage town of Sergiopolis (Resafe) and the fortresses of Halebiye and Qasr Ibn Wardan represent the continuing prosperity and strategic imperatives of the eastern Roman Empire.

The catastrophic defeat of the Emperor Heraclius at the Yarmuk in 636 brought Byzantine rule in Syria to an abrupt end. But the Omayyad rulers of Damascus learned much from the monuments they found, as the Great Mosque of their capital and the desert-bound Qasr al-Heir al-Sharqi demonstrate. Later phases of Muslim architecture are comprehensively represented at both Damascus and Aleppo. The citadel at Aleppo and Qalaat Najim, east of Aleppo, are both impressive even by the standards of the Crusader castles, three of the greatest of which – Krak des Chevaliers, Margat and Saone – are in Syria, while the souks of Aleppo even now take the visitor into a palpably medieval world, and some of the nourias of Hama built or rebuilt under the Ayyubids remain in service. The Mamelukes left many monuments in Damascus, while the Ottomans, who took Syria from them in 1516, built numerous religious foundations and khans there. The most beautiful early Ottoman buildings in Syria are perhaps Sinan's Tekkiye Mosque at Damascus and the al-Adeliye Mosque at Aleppo. The great builders of the eighteenth century were pashas of the Azem family, notably Assad al-Azem, whose palaces at Hama and Damascus are among the more memorable buildings of their time in Syria. The nineteenth century contributed less, and Ottoman control of Syria came to an end in 1918. The succeeding phase of French rule was in many ways unhappy. But it led to notable archaeological and restoration projects, and even now the great museum at Damascus has very much the air of a French institution.

My selection of places in this book is perhaps self-indulgent, reflecting as it does a wish to see as many major monuments in their proper contexts as is practical in a limited time. The Jezira gets short shrift, as few sightseers have an inexhaustible appetite for tells, however nobly these rise above their landscapes, and only the very committed would think the early bridge over the Tigris at Ain Divan *vaut le détour*, even if there were not frontier complications. I am conscious of other omissions: the Roman house at Inkhil, which I have not seen but which could easily be added to the circuit suggested in the Ledja; Jebel Seis, deep in the desert; Tell Nebi Mend, the ancient Qadesh, which I failed to find in uncompromising fog; and Qatna, which will be more visited when the treasures found there are on permanent exhibition at Homs, but which at the moment makes few concessions to the tourist. Most monuments in Syria are readily accessible, and the curious can with little difficulty gain access to many of the early houses of Damascus and Aleppo, some of which have recently been restored as hotels or for institutional use.

Syria pays a price for her prosperity. The record of her archaeological service is exemplary, and much recent restoration of the great monuments has the merit of being readily detectable. Less attention has been given to context. At Aleppo plans to cut roads through swathes of the ancient city have been withdrawn and necessary work has been done on innumerable buildings, both there and in the walled city at Damascus, where the future of the old housing in the medieval suburbs is, however, less secure. In cities that have been constantly redeveloped over millennia jarring juxtapositions are, of course, inevitable.

These are less acceptable elsewhere, for something of the appeal of many of the great monuments has been sacrificed. Hotel development at Palmyra calls for restraint. And hotels on prominent ridges near both Saone and Krak des Chevaliers do not enhance the settings of these most magical of castles. The hills inland from Tartus have sprouted a rash of unsightly villas, and more disfigure the Hauran. Quarrying now affects the context of a number of the 'dead cities'. The landscape once abused can never be reclaimed; one can only hope that the Syrian authorities come to recognize that rigorous planning control would serve both their country's recreational needs and its long-term interest as a destination for sustained tourism, before more irrevocable damage is done. Enthusiasm, too, can come at a price. The monument to the President outside the theatre at Bosra does no one any credit, while the new concrete terrace before the Temple of Helios at Qanawat is an unwelcome distraction. What, however, is very welcome is the increasing interest on the part of Syrian sightseers in their monuments, which promises well for the future of these.

Syria has been well served in print, as Marius Kociejowski's *Syria Through Writer's Eyes* (London, 2008) reminds us. Robin Fedden's *Syria* (London, 1946) remains the most compelling general account of the country and its major monuments. Ross Burns's comprehensive *Monuments of Syria: An Historical Guide* (London and New York, 1994) is altogether indispensable: this has led me to many less familiar sites, and is equally invaluable for its systematic references to earlier authorities, not least the indefatigable Professor H.C. Butler. Gertrude Bell and Freya Stark both wrote illuminatingly about places in Syria. Colin Thubron's *Mirror to Damascus* (London, 1967) is a penetrating, personal account of the city, about which Burns's *Damascus: A History* (London and New York, 2005) will surely remain the definitive work. Kevin Butcher's *Roman Syria and the Near East* (London, 2003) and Warwick Ball's *Syria: A Historical and Architectural Guide* (London, 1994) are both helpful to the non-specialist. Some early guidebooks continue to be of service. Thus early editions of

Murray's *Syria and Palestine* are informative about the Ledja. And without D. Kennedy and D. Riley's *Rome's Desert Frontier from the Air* (London, 1990) I might not have learnt of such sites as Khan al-Manquora.

The independent sightseer will need more recent guidebooks. On my first visit, at the end of the First Gulf War in 1991, I came to be properly grateful to John Hemming for insisting on lending me his copy of Lonely Planet's *Jordan and Syria* (1997). Ivan Mannheim's *Footprint Syria & Lebanon Handbook* (Bristol, 2001) is in a class of its own.

When planning a programme it is as well to remember that museums and some public monuments in Syria are closed on Tuesdays. Some mosques, even in major cities, are only open at prayer times. There are obvious places where the tourist will wish to stay: Damascus, Bosra, Palmyra, Deir al-Zor, Raqqa perhaps, Aleppo, Hama, Tartus or Safita. Parking will be a problem only in Aleppo and Damascus.

I am indebted to the many people in Syria who have treated me with unfailing generosity: to Georges and Miriam Antaki in Aleppo; to Mark and Halla Cochrane for wise advice in 1991 and subsequently; to the late Mr Mazloumian, and to his widow and son Arman, at the Baron Hotel; to Edouard de Pazzis, who in the week that he was my passenger in 1991 prevailed upon me to take the rusting boat to Arwad; to Taco Dibbits, the ideal travelling companion for nearly a fortnight in 2009; and to Ulrich Bormann for his help and guidance in so many matters. Only those who know my handwriting will fully understand how grateful I am to Rania Konstantinidou for transcribing much of my text. I am also grateful to Emil Joachim and his colleagues of Richard Caplan, who have made the best of my snapshots, and to John Nicoll, Andrew Dunn and Anne Askwith of Frances Lincoln.

1. DAMASCUS

Muhammad chose not to go to Damascus, as he did not wish to have a foretaste of paradise. The modern visitor, who arrives by air and is confronted by a city that has long since burst out of the girdle of its walls, may not at first find it easy to understand Damascus's hold on the historical imagination. The city to which St Paul rode so overconfidently owed her existence to the Barada, which carved its course eastwards through the hills and brought life to the inland plain, watering the Ghouta to the east of the city, source of the fruit for which it was famed, which still makes so dramatic a contrast with the desert beyond.

Damascus wears the marks of age. Dimashqa, first mentioned in the mid-third millennium BC and subsequently controlled by the Aramaens, and by Assyria and Babylon and Persia, has left its trace in the perceptible tell near the centre of the walled town, so much of which still bears the imprint of the plan imposed upon it after Alexander the Great took control in 332 BC. Rome won Damascus in 64 BC, although she accepted a strong Nabatean presence for roughly ninety years until AD 54. Thereafter the city benefited from the long years of Roman and Byzantine stability, which were brought to an abrupt end with the Arab victory of 636. In 661 Damascus became the capital of the fifth Caliph, al-Maowiya, whose Umayyad Empire was to endure for ninety years and saw the construction of the Great Mosque, which replaced the Byzantine cathedral that had in turn been created within the Roman reconstruction of the earlier Temple of Jupiter-Haddad.

The Umayyads' successors, the Abbasids, moved their capital to Baghdad, heralding a decline in the fortunes of Damascus. But these were later revived as a direct result of the Crusades. The dynamic Nur ad-Din seized Damascus in 1154: his son Saladin (1176–93) was the great champion of the Muslim cause; but his Ayyubid successors were not of the same stamp. In 1260 the Mamelukes under Sultan Baibars took control. Damascus became their second capital; and numerous Islamic foundations date from their period. But internal division and Mongol incursions progressively sapped the power of the Mamelukes, and, in 1516, Syria fell to the Ottomans. Damascus became the seat of a governor and numerous buildings testify to a continuing prosperity, owed partly to the city's position on the route of the Haj. Although outranked as a trading centre by Aleppo, Damascus remained a significant market, as the impressive khans of the Ottoman period show. Turkish rule ended abruptly on 1 October 1918 when the Allied army reached Damascus. Despite the offer of the throne to King Feisal, Syria was mandated to France at Versailles, and only became independent in 1946. Since then the growth of Damascus, already accelerating, has increased exponentially from a population of 300,000 to one of over 2,500,000.

The walls of Damascus enclosed a roughly oval area to the south of the Barada. At the north-western extremity is the rectangular citadel on the site of the Roman fort. The western section of the citadel walls has been reconstructed, but much of the medieval building survives to the north, and the north-east tower of 1209 is of imposing scale. The complex, which served as a prison until 1985, is being restored. Much work has recently been done on the surviving sections of the city wall, the most rewarding stretch of which is to the east of the citadel.

Just to the south of the citadel – on the line of the city wall – is the entrance to the Suq al-Hamidiye, now marked by a large poster of President Assad with the words: 'I believe in Syria.' The suq, or souk, lined with shops and protected from the sun by a metal roof, is the successor of the processional approach to the great Temple of Jupiter. Moneychangers and shopkeepers compete for the tourist's attention; and it is all but impossible to resist the ice cream of Messrs Bardaz. The souk turns slightly and ahead – best viewed perhaps from a curiosity shop high on the left – is the propylaeum, with a great arch set within a triangular pediment borne on tall Corinthian columns. This marked the entrance to the outer enclosure, the peribolos, of the temple. Beyond is what survives of the fourth-century arcade – which originally sheltered a market – leading to the western portal of the temenos, or inner enclosure, of the Roman temple. The Roman pantheon was inclusive, and at Damascus as elsewhere the Romans simply absorbed the deity of their predecessors. Thus the Semitic Haddad was subsumed by the Roman Jupiter, and the early shrine to the former at the centre of the temenos became one of the great pilgrimage centres of Roman Syria. With the adoption of Christianity, the temple was transformed into a cathedral, dedicated to St John the Baptist. This survived for some decades after the Arab conquest, sharing the precinct with the original mosque built against the south wall of the enclosure.

The lower courses of the wall, with large blocks of stone, are Roman, but there is much later work above. The eighteen pilasters give movement and shadow to what would otherwise be a monolithic mass, despite the drama of the minarets of the temple's successor, the Great Mosque. The temenos was rectangular, measuring some 100 metres/109 yards on the west and the east – originally the main approach – and 150 metres/165 yards to the north and south. The western Bab al-Barid is now reserved for the faithful, but do not miss the splendid bronze doors of 1416.

The tourist now gets a ticket in a building just to the north of the mosque and enters this by the Bab al-Amara, going into the vast enclosure of the courtyard of the Umayyad Mosque constructed for the Caliph al-Walid between 708 and 714–15. Opposite is the Great Prayer Hall of the mosque, with a raised central transept. This extends for the full length of the court. The other sides of the court are lined with arcades incorporating ancient columns. The sunlight glances almost too fiercely on

The Great Mosque.

the white marble paving, a late addition; and it is indeed in the afternoon that the courtyard is at its most spellbinding, with children playing and the constant *va et vien* of Near Eastern life.

The Caliph was evidently a perfectionist, and while time has not been kind to his great monument, something of the radiance of its design and execution can still be experienced. Originally both the façade of the prayer hall and the arcades were clothed in mosaic, for which craftsmen were summoned from as far as Byzantium. But the Umayyads envisaged decoration wholly unlike the hieratic expressions of faith found in a Byzantine cathedral. The mosaics of the mosque celebrated a very different kind of heaven, a paradise of green trees, of palaces and pavilions and clusters of more modest buildings set in gold. Most has been lost and much that is now in place is new. But the brilliance of the original can be seen in the well-protected west vestibule, in the darker sections on the outer wall of the transept of the mosque and above all in the less-restored sections of the extraordinary flowing landscape watered by a Barada of the imagination on the back wall of the western portico. Beautiful as the mosaics are in their own right, one is equally struck by the way that these relate to the fabric of the mosque, so that trees seem to sprout naturally between arches and to grow from the very structure. There are more mosaics on the elegant treasury, raised on classical columns, near the west end of the courtyard.

The mosque is best entered from the door from the western vestibule. The Umayyad plan survives. Three aisles intersect with the central transept, which emphasizes the mirhab, which in turn was aligned on Mecca. But much of the structure was altered after a devastating fire of 1893. The wooden ceiling of the transept and the six early windows at the ends of this are the only original elements to survive.

Return to the courtyard and linger there, taking in the three minarets. To the north, by the Bab al-Amara, is the ninth-century Tower of the Bride, the upper section of which is of the twelfth century. The tall

Tower of Jesus at the south-east corner was built in 1247, although the superstructure is Ottoman, while the south-western tower, Madhanat al-Gharbiye, is an enchanting Mameluke addition of 1488, built for Sultan Qait Bey. Leaving by the Bab al-Amara – and passing another stretch of fourth-century arcade – it is worth turning right, through an area of old housing, keeping to the right to follow as far as possible the outer temenos wall. The lane emerges just east of the Bab Jairun. There is a spectacular view up to the Tower of Jesus before you turn to follow the southern wall of the temenos, with its blocked Roman entrance.

The area round the Umayyad Mosque is rich in monuments. To the north-west, opposite one another on a narrow lane, are two fine madrasas: on the left is the Madrasa Adeilye, completed in 1222–3, now used by the National Library. The outstanding feature is the decoration of the entrance, with a pendant keystone. This clearly challenged the architect employed by the son of Sultan Baibars in 1277 to build his father's mausoleum, the Madrasa Zahiriye. Black and yellow stone and marble were used; and the stalactite-like muqarnas are handled with extraordinary refinement.

South of the mosque and the Suq al-Hamidiye, in the heart of the busy market area, are many of the khans which are among the most characteristic monuments of Ottoman Damascus. Most of the more atmospheric are still in use, for example the Khan al-Zait off Straight Street. By far the grandest is the Khan Assad Pasha, built in 1752 by the governor of Aleppo, Assad Pasha al-Azem. This has recently been restored, although the central dome has not been replaced.

Two blocks north of the khan, a street on the right leads to the Beit al-Azem, the great palace built by the Pasha in 1749–52. This is by far the largest of the palaces of Ottoman Damascus, which explains why King Feisal used it in 1919. Damaged by fire in 1925, the palace was later the French Institute. After the Second World War Prince Ali Khan proposed to restore it to residential use, but in 1951 it was acquired by the Syrian government and now serves as the Museum of 'Popular Arts and Traditions'. Exhibits include a baldachin for a camel used on the Haj. Many of the main rooms retain elements of their original decoration, but the appeal of the place owes more to the wide courtyard with its orange trees, and to the views of the Tower of Jesus.

A block to the south of the Khan Assad Pasha, the Suq al-Bazuriye intersects with Straight Street – 'the street called straight' – which was the decumanus of Roman Damascus. Follow this eastwards. After some 300 metres/328 yards there are the remains of a Roman arch, the Bab al-Kanisa, at the point where the street crossed the cardo maximus. The Christian quarter was ahead to the left, that of the Jews on the right. Just before the gate a lane to the south leads, after 150 metres/160 yardsyards, to the turn to the Palais Dahdah. This eighteenth-century house was restored with great tact about sixty years ago. Still lived in by the Dahdah family, it retains the charm that so many of the other houses in the city, such as the Beit Nizam not far to the west, have lost as a result of over-zealous attention.

Straight Street continues eastwards to the Bab Sharqi. Drums from the colonnade that flanked the street lie beside this. The prosperity of the several churches that are near the street is reassuring; and so is the conviction of those now responsible for two visually not particularly rewarding shrines, the chapels of St Ananias and St Paul.

The area west of the Suq al-Hamidiye has been extensively developed. On the Sharia Jamal Pasha is the station of 1913, originally the terminus of the Hejaz Railway Line, which was intended for pilgrims on the Haj to Mecca, built in an appropriately national style. Further out, just south of the Shoukh al-Quwatli Street, is what is arguably the most beautiful complex of Ottoman Syria, the Tekkiye Mosque, designed by Sinan in 1553–4 for Sultan Suleiman the Magnificent, to serve pilgrims on the Haj. The domed mosque dominates a courtyard with arcaded ranges that served as a khan, some of which have been in somewhat incongruous use as a military museum. Trees enhance the charm of the place. To the east, built for the Sultan's heir, Selim II, is the Madrasa Selimiye, now largely in service as a souk for craftsmen. A certain air of decay contributes to the appeal of the place.

The souk no doubt benefits from its proximity to the National Museum, a block to the west. Begun in 1936 and enlarged subsequently, this should be visited, if possible, before embarking on a tour of the country, as a knowledge of the collection, however slight, adds immeasurably to the experience of many archaeological sites.

You enter the museum through the spectacular gate from Qasr al-Heir al-Gharbi, which reveals how well the Umayyads could digest the varied styles – Sasanian, metropolitan Byzantine and local – on which they drew. To achieve a chronological survey of the collections, turn right and proceed to the small room of objects from Ugarit (1600–1300 BC), including an ivory panel with insistent profiles that recall those of Egypt, a horn decorated with a naked woman, an ivory table top and a tablet with an alphabet. In the next room there are items from other Bronze Age sites and from Ebla, the latter including a ritual basin. The finds from Mari are particularly rich, with treasure from an urn excavated in 1965, inlaid friezes and foundation blocks. Particularly fine is the gypsum statuette of a singer, Ur-Nanshe, with huge eyes and an almost humorous twist to the mouth.

At this point in the circuit, return to the central hall and cross to the east wing. To the left are objects from the Hauran. The basalt statuary tends to be crude but there is a fine mosaic from Shahba. More memorable is an exceptional marble sarcophagus with a relief of Greek warships bearing down on naked Trojans on the shore. Among the smaller works near by are glass vessels in the form of fish, an ivory casket cover with the Three Graces – which one hopes was presented to someone equally well favoured – and a statuette from Hama that has been identified as of Aspasia, which is most remarkable for the sense of weight in the drapery. Near by is a finely cut small limestone relief of a woman of the Taai family from Palmyra, which is of much greater refinement than the portraits in the reconstructed Hypogeum of Yarhai, to which steps descend. Particularly fascinating, in the Palmyra Gallery to the right of the main corridor, are the textiles found in the tombs – fragments of Chinese silks, of painted and printed cottons, and of embroidered linen – for the Palmyrenes were as exacting buyers of exotic fabrics as any modern addict of the souks.

In a separate building, across a courtyard and not always open, is the reconstruction of the synagogue from Dura Europos. That a Jewish synagogue of about AD 150 was decorated with biblical scenes comes as a very considerable surprise. The murals are rather crude, but this does not detract from their energy or diminish the fascination of their blend of Parthian and Western influences.

The Byzantine section of the museum is relatively modest. But there is a beautiful detached twelfth-century mural of an angel from Qara; and silver of the same period found at Resafe repays attention: a chalice with a roundel of Christ, a pattern with a frieze of running rabbits and roundels of birds.

The Islamic collections are in the west wing. The star among the pottery from Raqqa is the blue-glaze-streaked statuette of a horseman of a strongly Asiatic type, who defends himself from a serpentine dragon that has curled round the front left leg of his mount. In the following gallery is an almost equally memorable jar of turquoise green, with reliefs of two horsemen hunting in a wood, which must also reflect the Mongol occupation. Other items stand out: stucco and a mosque lamp from Meskene, a flask with a Mameluke blazon, a bowl decorated with a woman seated as though she was curled up, pottery in blue and turquoise as well as later tiles from Damascus and Hama. But the display ends with a sorry anticlimax, the grotesque Damascene Hall, more eloquent of the taste of 1960 than that of the eighteenth century which it purports to represent.

There is much of architectural interest outside the walled city. The Salihiye district, on the flank of Mount Kassiun, a couple of kilometres/a mile or so to the north, was developed from the twelfth century. A remarkable sequence of medieval buildings survives. A circuit might begin at the Madrasa Maridaniye off Jisr al-Abiad Square, and continue uphill to follow the Madares Assad al-Din eastwards. The walk is particularly rewarding in the afternoon. Many of the Islamic buildings, and almost all the domed turbe, will be closed. But the façades hold the attention, and on Fridays the busy market adds colour. Opposite and just before the mausoleum of the Sufi Mohi al-Din Ibn al-Arabi, who died in 1240, is an unusual smaller building, the Imaret of Sultan Suleiman, designed by no less an architect than Sinan to supply bread for pilgrims to the mausoleum: remarkably this is still in use as a bakery. A turn to the left after 100 metres/110 yards leads to the Hanbila Mosque (1202–13), with a beautiful courtyard in which ancient columns were reused. One of the original elaborately sculpted windows of the façade of the mosque survives, and there is a fine mimbar in the prayer hall. Back on the main thoroughfare is the elegant Madrasa Sahibiye, built before 1245 by a sister of Saladin. Her nephew, Emir Rukn ad-Din Mankuris, founded the Madrasa Rukniye a couple of hundred metres/yards further on. The impact of the front, with fine Kufic lettering, is somewhat marred by a new minaret.

The area immediately to the north of the walls has charm of a different kind, with modest houses lining the Barada. Much of the original street pattern survives. And roughly north of Bab al-Salaam is what must be the most appealing Mameluke minaret of Damascus. The prayer hall of the Mosque of al-Aqsab, which was reconstructed in 1408, is memorable only for the mirhab of polychrome marbles, but the square minaret, predominantly of pale stone, is distinguished for the inspired used of bands of black blocks, and for the double windows near the top, which are almost Gothic in pattern.

The ground south-west of the walled city was also developed under the Mamelukes. South of the west entrance to the Suq al-Hamidiye, on Zaghlul Street, are two handsome Ottoman mosques: on the right, often closed, that of Darwish Pasha (1572–5), with a long façade to the street; and beyond, to the left, the Mosque of Sinan Pasha, completed in 1590. The minaret is of glazed brick, in greens of varying depth with bands of turquoise; there are excellent tiles on the façade of the prayer hall, which in turn is most appealing. The road runs into Midan Street, the artery of the Midan quarter, which was developed in medieval and Ottoman times to serve pilgrims on the Haj. Not everyone will relish the 3-kilometre/2-mile walk, but it is certainly worth going as far as the Mausoleum of Arak, the modest front of which is a perfect statement of the refinement of mid-fourteenth-century Mameluke architecture. The mosque is built of alternating courses of grey and pale brown stone, the central band being of black, while grey and pale brown blocks alternate in the framing of the three circular windows. The arch above the portal is decorated in honeycomb; over this there is a slightly pointed shell, surmounted by an intricate design, with turquoise and white tiles inset in the stone.

Damascus was celebrated for its oasis, watered by the Barada. Few tourists now visit the Ghouta, to the east of the city. But despite much unappealing development, it is still possible to see why this was so admired. Parties from the city visit the orchards in the spring and sit on plastic chairs round the trees to savour the blossom. Near the eastern extremity of the oasis, where the water has been exhausted, is the small town of Haran al-Awamid. The modest mosque incorporates the spoil of Nabatean and Roman buildings. Near by three fine columns, one still with its Ionic capital of a temple that was originally placed on a high podium, rise above a mud-brick house that has been wrapped around the remains of the substructure. The columns impress far more than would be the

The Mosque of Sinan Pasha.

case if the remains had been cleared and sanitized. And the inhabitants of the house are hospitably tolerant of the passing sightseer.

Haran al-Awamid: basalt columns of the temple.

2. EZRAA

On the western edge of the Ledja, known in antiquity as Trachonitis, off the motorway to Amman some 80 kilometres/50 miles south of Damascus, is the modern town of Ezraa. Some 2 kilometres/1 mile north of its central junction are two very remarkable early churches, which testify to the fervour of the Byzantine town of Andrea Zorava.

Mar Georgis, as an inscription above the central door states, was built in 515, succeeding 'a lodging place of demons', evidently a pagan shrine. The black basalt structure is rectangular. The exterior, despite the three fine door-cases on the west front and others on the lateral façades, does not prepare one for the ingenuity of the internal plan. The central octagon rests on six-sided piers, the two short inner faces of which are cut back as in the undersides of chevrons. The masonry rises from these to become a circular drum lit by eight windows. The dome above is modern, but the ambulatory retains the original corbelled ceilings. The corners of the square are treated as semi-circular chapels. To the east, the chancel is flanked by lateral rooms, also with corbelled ceilings, above which are further chambers. The icons and other fittings are not particularly distinguished, but contribute to the atmosphere of a building that continues to be used by the Syrian Orthodox church.

A little to the south of the Mar Georgis is what remains of an Ayyubid mosque. The courtyard is a chaos of basalt blocks, including a fragment of a Byzantine door jamb with vine decoration. The open prayer hall is of five bays. Not far to the east is the second of the churches of Ezraa, Mar Elias, the church of the Greek Catholics. An inscription establishes a date of 542. The plan, most unusually for Syria, is cruciform. The interior is much restored, but the fabric is substantially original; recently the generosity of a parishioner has helped the enthusiastic priest, Father Elias, to undertake

necessary repairs. The west door and that to the small courtyard on the south are of interest: the shape of the lateral blocks flanking the oculi above both evokes the wings of a dove and thus alludes to the Holy Spirit; and several early inscriptions are set into the walls.

Mar Georgis and Mar Elias are remarkable survivals and their future seems secure, for Ezraa is still inhabited by several hundred Christian families. These have remained in their town despite over a millennium of Muslim domination. Their Christianity is not lightly borne. As I pass the church, a youth crosses himself while, when Father Elias unlocks his eponymous church for the visitor, a couple of adolescents come in to pray. On my first visit, on a very cold morning just after Christmas, the strains of 'O come all ye faithful' rose from a half-buried house near by.

Mar Georgis, the Church of St George.

3. BOSRA

The Hauran, the ancient Auranitis, which included the Jebel al-Arab and much of the plain to the west, was an area of great prosperity under Roman rule, when like the Nile delta and certain parts of Asia Minor it was a major centre of grain production. There had been a town at Bosra since the Bronze Age. The successor of this passed from the Selucids to Judas Maccabeus in 163 , before falling to the Nabateans, whose capital it was from 70 until the imposition of Roman rule by Trajan in 106. Bosra then became, as Nova Trajana Bostra, the capital of the Provincia Arab. Hadrian visited the city, Alexander Severus nominated this as a colony and Philip the Arab, whose family came from nearby Shahba, elevated it to metropolitan status. Later Bosra was the seat of a powerful bishopric, where Monophysite leanings were favoured by the local rulers, the Ghassanids. Muhammad visited the place as a merchant and apparently sought advice from a Nestorian monk, Bahira. In 632 Bosra, which was on their direct route to central Syria, was the first major Byzantine town to fall to the Arabs. Subsequently changing circumstances eroded the agricultural economy of the Hauran. The Crusaders raided Bosra in 1147 and 1151, and later it was threatened by rivalry between the rulers of Damascus and Cairo. The Ayyubids refortified the theatre from 1202 and their work was continued for Sultan Baibars in 1261, in the wake of the first Mongol invasion. As the theatre owes its remarkable condition to its being wrapped within the Muslim defences, so the preservation of these is due the fact that they became progressively less important as the main route to the south shifted westwards.

The theatre.

However much the visitor to Bosra knows about the second-century theatre, the first impression of the massive rectangular towers of the Ayyubid fortress breaking forward from the original structure comes as a surprise. The entrance leads across a moat to a massive tower built out from the original stage building. A gallery links the three northern towers. From this, through one of the two internal courtyards that the Ayyubids heightened by a storey, you reach the western entrance to the orchestra. On the left is the stage building. While the structure of this survives to full height, we can only imagine the richness of the inlaid marbles and the lavish entablatures on three tiers from the beautiful Corinthian columns of the lower level. Much work was done in the major programme begun in 1947. The same is true of the upper section of the auditorium. But otherwise the latter is astonishingly well preserved. There was room for 6,000 spectators to sit, and the seats were disposed in 37 rows, 14 below, 18 in the second tier and 5 above. The sides of the benches flanking the stairways in the top row of the second tier are richly carved. And numerous game boards cut in the pavement remind us that the Romans and later inhabitants knew well how to amuse themselves.

The upper courtyard contrived by the Ayyubids behind the stage building is now an open-air museum. Among the sculpture is a most spirited relief of a bearded man with wild hair. There are numerous architectural fragments cut in the unyielding basalt. But in fierce sunlight it is difficult to appreciate the mosaics, of such subjects as dogs hunting hares and peasants harvesting dates. The very Spartan hostel in the north tower has now been closed, but one can still walk round the upper level, from which there are views over the Roman town and southwards to the large hippodrome.

On leaving the theatre, turn left to head for the heart of the Roman town. To the left are the substantial ruins of the Southern Baths, set back from the decumanus, the main street, just to the west of the intersection with the road that ran to the north gate, which was marked by a nymphaeum, of which four Corinthian columns survive. The decumanus was lined with Ionic columns, some of which remain in place. Head west, pausing at the first junction on the left by the monumental arch to the II Cyrenaica Legion, set up early in the third century but altered at an early date. Further on is the cryptoporticus, a large covered warehouse, ventilated by narrow slits in the steps of what was once the portico above. The street ends 200 metres/218 yards beyond at the second-century West Gate, flanked by towers enriched with pilasters framing pedimented niches. As with the Damascus Gate at Palmyra, there was an ovoid forum within the gate. Walking back on my first visit I was ever more aware that my pleasure in Bosra was enhanced by the fact that it has not been sanitized and that many of the houses built of robbed material are still in use.

Turn left by the cryptoporticus. On the right after some 200 metres/218 yards, among a scattering of trees, is the small Mosque of al-Khider. This was reconstructed with recycled material including basalt doors in 1133. A lane runs eastwards to the Mosque of Umar, built in 720 but greatly enlarged for the Ayyubids. The entrance is on the east, on the main road from the North Gate. The now tin-roofed courtyard is flanked by double arcades and flows into the wider double-aisled prayer hall. Columns and capitals were appropriated, many of the finer, of a yellow marble, for use in the prayer hall. The complex was originally linked with a souk, the successor of the Roman marketplace that had been immediately to the south. Immediately opposite the mosque is the recently restored Hammam Manjak of 1372, which is particularly ingenious in plan.

A path to the east leads to the basilica, a third-century public building that was adapted as a church and may owe its survival to Muslim reverence for the monk Bahira. Some 250 metres/273 yards along the lane that passes this, just within the line of the town walls, is the Mabrak Mosque, built in three sections from 1136 and still a place of pilgrimage.

South of the basilica are the ruins of the considerable cathedral, dedicated in 512–13. The circular central space vied with that of the original

Haghia Sophia at Constantinople, and was set within a square with exedras which helped to bear the weight of the dome. The plan was thus similar to that at Ezraa, but on a vastly different scale. Leaving the modest Fatima Mosque on the right, head south for the Nabatean Arch, built in the second century, perhaps as the entrance to the compound of an earlier temple. The design is agreeably eccentric. The track through the arch curls past other basalt structures, of which the most considerable – to the south – was regarded by Professor Butler as the residence of the governor of the Provincia Arabia. Behind this is the huge rectangular cistern, the Birket al-Haj, measuring more than 120 by 150 metres/390 by 490 feet, which is overlooked by the Ayyubid Mosque of Abu al-Feda. Here, as in my experience nowhere else in Syria, one should be wary of pickpocketing adolescents.

The Mosque of Abu al-Feda reflected in the Roman cistern.

4. QANAWAT

Qanawat is first recorded in the first century AD and was until the reign of Trajan, with Damascus and places now in Jordan including Pella and Gadara, one of the cities of the Decapolis. Later Qanawat was transferred from the province of Syria to that of Arabia. Under the Byzantines it became the seat of a bishop. Decline set in with the Arab conquest and the town only began to revive during the last century.

Despite new development, Qanawat remains a site of extraordinary charm. This owes much to the beauty of its position, raised on a shelf on the western flank of the Jebel el-Arab, some 5 kilometres/3 miles from Suweida, now the bustling provincial capital, where most of the buildings recorded by the indefatigable J.L. Porter, D.D., in his *Giant Cities of Bashan* of 1865, and other early travellers were torn down just over a hundred years ago when the Ottomans needed material for a new barracks. As a result we can judge the prosperity of the Roman Soada only from the scale of the extant fragment of the front of a huge fourth-century cathedral, now severed from an eroded odeon by the modern highway. Altogether more rewarding is the excellent new museum on the road to Qanawat. Rich in sculpture from sites throughout the Hauran, this is most memorable for a group of third-century mosaics from Shahba, of which a *Diana and Actaeon* and a *Birth and Toilet of Venus* are particularly fine.

The road climbs. And one is at once aware of the fertility of the ground. The Temple of Helios stands on a platform to the left, overlooking the plain. The readily reusable material has long since been taken, but a cluster of columns gives a sense of the elegance of the design. Beyond, the road descends to the centre of the modern town on the left bank of the deep Wadi al-Ghar. Crossing to the opposite side of the stream, one can reach a small odeon and a nymphaeum on foot. But the main monuments, known as the Saraya, are just above the town, reached by either of the roads to the south of the central junction.

The main buildings in this remarkable complex, both of basilica form, date from the second century AD. But what we now see is the result of their modification for Christian use. The western structure may have been intended as a praetorium and was orientated to serve as a church in the fifth century, when the imposing and richly decorated façade was built, reusing earlier material. Immediately to the east was a long colonnaded courtyard, of the third century. This was later intersected by an impressive façade with three finely carved doors to form a substantial public monument, which in turn was orientated when it was transformed into a church. The masonry is of consistently high quality. And the buildings' setting among trees is particularly happy.

A hundred metres/109 yards to the south-west, beyond a cistern of which the ribs of the vault are exposed, is the second-century Temple of Zeus. Little more than the podium is in place. The temple was beside the processional route to the early Sanctuary of Baal-Shamir at Sia. To reach this, follow the road past the Saraya. After 3 kilometres/2 miles the road turns left before a ridge and then bends back to climb this. Stop by the first buildings and walk to the right.

Originally a Semitic high place, the shrine at Sia was developed by the Nabateans in successive phases from about 50 BC. A sequence of courts can be made out and there was one main temple and at least two subsidiary ones. The ruins, alas, were ruthlessly quarried by the Turks when they built their barracks at Suweida. But the promontory site, overlooking a relatively undisturbed valley, is most appealing. And among the chaos of battered blocks of basalt that the Ottomans rejected are tantalizing fragments of friezes with leaf motifs and of carved consoles.

The visitor with time may wish to see three small but elegant Roman temples in nearby villages off the main road from Suweida to Shahba.

The two at Atil are very similar in both design and detail. One of the angle pilasters of their ruinous counterpart at Salim somehow continues to defy gravity.

The Saraya.

5. SHAHBA

The approach to Shahba is dominated by the volcanic cone of Tell Shihon. The town lies between the Hauran and the Ledja, but it was not for strategic or commercial reasons that it was laid out in the brief half decade from 244 AD. For Shahba was the project, in Burns's words, of the 'local boy made good', Philip the Arab, who became Emperor in that year and wished his town to have all the amenities of a Roman city.

Work proceeded quickly. Town walls were laid out, with monumental gateways at the ends of the two main streets that intersected at the centre of the urban grid; and public buildings were erected at considerable speed. These are concentrated around the forum, to the west of the central crossing. The large paved forum is dominated by the rather gaunt and overweening palace, with an outsize exedra, which was perhaps intended for the display of statues of the Emperor's ancestors. To the south is the exceptionally well-preserved temple, which may have been dedicated to Philip's father, Julianus Marinus. External decoration is limited to the chaste corner pilasters; but the interior contained niches for more dynastic sculptures and was lavishly adorned with marbles, as holes for attachments show. Behind the temple is the theatre. This too is relatively intact. But by the standard of Bosra it is, with a diameter of some 42 metres/138 feet, rather modest. And the bare unyielding basalt is monotonous to the eye.

More ambitious in scale were the baths, some 300 metres/328 yards to the east. To reach these from the main crossroad, head south and take the first road to the left. The unexpected size of the complex is matched by the ingenuity of the plan. In the south block there were three immense

The theatre.

rooms, with two apodyteria flanking the frigidarium, linking with the two circular caldaria at the centre of the wider northern range. Behind these was an unusually long tepidarium with absidal ends; and there were two additional rooms at either side. The masonry was of consistently fine quality, and concrete, which was less heavy than stone, was used for the vaults and domes: this can be examined at close quarters by climbing the stairs in the eastern wall of the frigidarium. The internal walls were faced with marble. Work may have been halted abruptly on the Emperor's death in 249.

Across the road is the small but most rewarding museum. There is some sculpture, but it is for the mosaics that one returns. Found in a house of the second quarter of the fourth century, these are as fine of any of their date from the Eastern Empire. The finest perhaps is a large head of Tethys, the marine goddess, with a serpent coiled about her neck and fish in her hair, her nose, cheek and chin flushed with red, her eyes alert, her mouth just open. Rarely does the art of mosaic achieve such vitality. Similar in style and almost as refined in quality is the scene rather charmingly labelled 'Orpheus the famous Greek musician and singer', in which animals and birds listen, and the snake hanging from the tree is open mouthed.

6. SHAQQA

Shaqqa, the Byzantine Maximianopolis, is a mere 8 kilometres/5 miles east of Shahba, but few tourists trouble to search out its monuments. While Shahba was planned as an imperial statement, its neighbour was an unpretending yet prosperous town, drawing on the resources of an area where arable farming was highly profitable. Shaqqa ranked as a colony of Rome and was, under the Byzantines, the seat of a bishopric.

The ground slopes gently to the south. The visitor's first impression is not favourable, as recent development has impinged on the Roman buildings. The most substantial of these is the palace, which fronts a square at the heart of the modern town. The central portal is lavishly decorated; and the buttresses of the southern wall are both functional and visually effective. Throughout the basalt masonry is of consistently fine quality. The forecourt leads to a well-preserved room with a corbelled ceiling supported by transverse arches. Behind this was a considerably larger hall, the roof of which has fallen. On the south side of the square is the substantial remnant of the façade of what has plausibly been identified as a pre-Christian basilica.

Higher up in the town is a handsome domed chamber, now known as al-Maabed. This has been put to service by the Druzes, to whom the resettlement of Shaqqa as of much of the Jebel al-Arab is largely due. There is a fine pedimented external niche, and the interior, with four columns, is equally elegant. More easily found, just beyond the eastern fringe of the modern town, is the monastery. This is dominated by a handsome tower. To the right of this is the lower section of the front of the church. The larger central door is still in use, and two transverse arches of the nave are intact, but the rest of the building has been greatly altered.

A minor road runs from Shaqqa to the north-west, reaching the main route to Damascus at al-Matunah. In the first significant village, Hit, the Roman Eitha, there are a villa of two storeys and a large reservoir of a type frequently found throughout the Hauran. Hayyat, the next village, is yet more rewarding. Here also there is an open cistern, its walls lined with regular courses of small stones. Near by there is an unusually big house, again of two storeys and still in use, with twenty-six rooms round a courtyard. An inscription of 578 states that the builder was Flavios Seos, who clearly did well in the service of the Ghassanid ruler, Almundaros.

More accessible is one of the most fascinating smaller buildings of Roman Syria, the Kalybe. This belongs to a small group of shrines peculiar to the northern Hauran. That at Umm az-Zaytun is datable to 282 and referred to as 'sacred kalybe' (the Greek *kalybe* means 'hut'); the rectangular shrine at Hayyat is no doubt of the same period and can thus have only been in use for a few generations before the adoption of Christianity. The entrance is to the north. Steps from either side give access to the arched entrance to the raised central cult chamber, which was originally domed. To the right of the arch on the outer wall there is a wide niche. Adjoining the chamber at either end of the building were rooms on two storeys. A door on the right, which retains its basalt door, opened to the lower room, from which a narrow stair led to the upper level. It is unfortunate that a large new house has been erected beside a most unusual and satisfying monument.

The palace: buttresses on the south wall.

7. THE LEDJA

North-west of the Roman Auranitis, but within the larger area long known as the Hauran, lies a great lava field, the Ledja (from the Arabic for 'refuge'), which until the recent introduction of well-marked roads must have been among the most impenetrable areas of Syria. The Ledja has long been inhabited. Where it is practical to clear it, the soil is naturally fertile and many of the villages have developed around townships that grew up during the prosperous years of Roman rule and were abandoned after the Byzantine withdrawal; these were only resettled in the eighteenth century by the Druzes. The Ledja fascinated nineteenth-century visitors; and in the 1920s the broken terrain made it difficult for the French to suppress the Druze rebellion. Even now the country seems untamed. In spring, the black of the lava is intensified by the lush green of the grasses and by swathes of yellow flowers; a few orchards have been planted and there is a scattering of bushes and a rash of red poppies.

Beyond Shahba the road to Damascus passes to the right of a sequence of villages on the eastern fringe of the Ledja, of which Buraq, the Roman Berroka, is the most northerly. Among the modern houses are groups of early ones, many set within larger enclosures. The material is basalt, with extant roofs of blocks laid on corbels. Most of the walls are relatively crude, and some have clearly been altered. But numerous Byzantine inscriptions attest to the fervour of the original inhabitants.

A rewarding way to cross the Ledja is to turn off the Damascus road at Umm az-Zaytun, some 5 kilometres/3 miles north of Shahba. Here there are a number of houses of sophisticated construction, one with double-tiered colonnades. Near by is the relatively modest kalybe, or open shrine,

Dama: the pyramid.

built under Probus (276–82). From here a route to the north-west passes Majadil, which was on a Roman road, and Smeid, where the cella of a Roman temple with a fine door has been adapted as the village mosque. There are more early buildings in the next village, Waqim. A couple of kilometres/a mile further on, a side road to the right leads to Deir Dama. To the north-west of this scattered village is a particularly good group of early houses, which like their counterparts throughout the Ledja are readily distinguished by their black material from their modern rendered counterparts. The complex consists of a monastery with a church and a small chapel and numerous associated houses. Steps lead to upper floors and roofs. A dog chained on top of a modern house barks its disapproval of the intruder.

Returning to the 'main' road, turn right for Dama. Clearly visible to the north of the village is the remarkable step pyramid, set on a wave of lava, which at 15 metres/50 feet is by far the tallest ancient monument of the Ledja. This is clearly pre-Nabatean, but its precise date is not yet altogether clear. The pyramid is raised on a terrace entered from the west. The structure rises in two steps with tapering walls, the outer wrapped round the inner. Many of the blocks are of considerable size and those of the corners are carefully shaped. There were originally rooms in the upper structure, reached through a door on the east. From the top there are sweeping views – with the Hauran and the volcanic cones around Shahba to the east and the snow-clad Mount Hermon to the west. Fifty metres/54 yards south-east is the Temenos of Athena, with a richly decorated Nabatean door-case.

South-west of Dama are the villages of Jrèn and Lubben, the Byzantine Agraian. There are early houses in each, but Lubben is the more rewarding, with a number of façades of high quality, behind one of which is a fine room with transverse arches and five well-constructed recesses. There are two churches, the larger of 417. Other early buildings may be seen in villages near by, for example Harran to the south. One can perhaps tire of basalt walls. But the charm of the Ledja is what would draw one back, for development has been limited; and, unlike their neighbours in the jebel, the inhabitants of the area have thus far not sought to disfigure their birthright by constructing pretentious villas in unsuitable places. I hope that the authorities will give the whole area the degree of protection this so well deserves.

8. SEIDNAYA AND MAALULA

Two Christian enclaves have – more or less – survived on the eastern side of the Anti-Lebanon range within easy reach of Damascus.

The nearer is Seidnaya, where it is to be hoped that new building will not altogether diminish the impact of the towering Convent of Our Lady of Seidnaya which rises from an outcrop to the east of the town. The convent is said to have been founded by the Emperor Justinian. It came to enjoy considerable prestige as a place of pilgrimage, and pilgrims continued to visit Seidnaya – which remained under Muslim control – at the time of the Crusades. Even now the picture of the Virgin attributed to St Luke, concealed within a niche in the shrine, the 'Shagoura', is revered and not only by Christians.

The outcrop must always have been a prominent landmark. Just above the road, below the south wall of the monastery, is an unusually ambitious Roman tomb, with three pairs of admittedly very worn standing figures in shell niches above the entrance to the burial chamber. The inscriptions below in Greek establish a date of 178 AD. Higher up, ancient steps can be seen on the way to the low door of the monastery. This has been extensively reconstructed. The main church is not of particular distinction, although some of the icons repay attention. More interesting is the 'Shagoura'. This is approached through two rooms, in the second of which there is a good late icon, as well as many that are execrable. The shrine itself is candlelit and the custodians are suspicious of torches, which means that it is difficult to examine the icons. But some are clearly of exceptional quality: these include a representation of a saint prostrate before the Virgin against a background of buildings, and a small Virgin and Child with two tiny saints on the border. An icon of scenes from the Life of the Virgin, beginning with the Meeting of Joachim and Anna, is unusual

Seidnaya, tomb below the convent: niche with paired figures.

in composition, but no fewer than five panels of the Virgin and Child of the same pattern show how key a role traditional iconography had in the Syrian church.

In the village there are other shrines and churches. The most interesting is the small Church of St Peter by the roundabout. This is in a Roman structure, which was not significantly modified when it was transformed for Christian use. The continuing resilience of Christianity at Seidnaya is shown by the fact that a not insubstantial church is under construction. Another small church converted from a Roman building, the Monastery of Mar Thomas, is 2 kilometres/1 mile away.

Maalula is 26 kilometres/16 miles to the north. The village hangs above a narrow valley between two sections of the eroded cliff that marks the flank of the Anti-Lebanon. Until recently Aramaic was its language; and the name in Aramaic means 'entrance', supposedly referring to the steep and narrow gorge through which a path climbs from the village. The village itself boasts the large and unappealing Deir Mar Taqla and other modern churches. The antiquity of the place is attested by numerous rock cuttings visible from the road up the wider gorge south of the village. At the top of this, below another rupestrian complex, a turn to the right leads to Deir Mar Sarkis, the church of St Sergius. Here too reconstruction is in evidence. The small low door gives to a courtyard, in which only the arcade through which you enter is original. The church with three apses and a dome has a simple but satisfying stone screen: in the central apse there are three reused Ionic capitals of a very provincial standard. Icons are arranged above the screen and elsewhere in the church. The earliest are of the seventeenth century, but most are later, including a Madonna and Child and a Christ of 1813 by Michael of Crete, who must have had an almost Mughal interest in costume.

9. DEIR MAR MOUSA

There is no more atmospheric Christian site in Syria than the monastery of Mar Mousa, St Moses, an Ethiopian venerated by the Syrian Catholic Church.

The monastery is north-east of Nabk, a straggling town 81 kilometres/50 miles north of Damascus to the east of the motorway. The only sign in the town is not helpful, but once one is clear of this, the road is well marked. The monastery is set on a platform high up a gully that cuts into the escarpment, which falls away to the level desert. The original approach was from above, but now the visitor arrives on a side road below the monastery and climbs up a steep but well-graded path. The monastery rises from the cliff, looking as Robert Tewdwr Moss thought 'like an old fort' (*Cleopatra's Wedding Present*, London, 1997). The blank external walls reveal little, but other modern buildings near by attest to the revitalization of the monastery, which had been abandoned since the seventeenth century, by a visionary Italian priest, Paolo dell' Oglio, with the support of Syrian Catholics.

As one draws near, the crow of the monastery cockerel can be heard. Breathless perhaps after the ascent, the pilgrim must stoop to enter the low door. A passage leads to a terrace, now protected by an awning, with a memorable view downwards to the semi-desert. The land falls away in an eddy of low hills. The pattern of light changes as clouds blow past, but in the long, ruthless summers the prospect must be relentless.

The monastery was founded in the sixth century. The church is on the left side of the court. The relatively modest door does not prepare the visitor for what is in store. You find yourself in the right aisle of an eleventh-century church with an absidal nave separated by arcades from the two aisles. Only since the recent restoration, completed in 2003, has

the importance of the murals in the church become clear. These date largely from the eleventh and thirteenth centuries and are in a strongly linear local style. Among the earlier murals are the unevenly preserved scenes from the Life of Christ and the beautifully intertwined Samson and the Lion above the arcade in the right aisle. Stylistically close are two small compartments by the window in the apse of the left aisle: an angel advancing, his hands concealed by the patterned clothes hanging from his shoulders; and a bearded stylite on a thick red column with Ionic volutes, sensibly topped by a white fence to prevent his falling.

The most ambitious composition is the Last Judgement that fills the west wall of the nave and spreads to sections of the adjacent arcades. Conventionally resolved in tiers and on a deep slate-blue ground, the mural is energetic rather than refined. Flanking this above the arcades are equally well-preserved large representations of the Syrian equestrian saints, Sergius and Bacchus, in very stylized landscapes. The painters responsible for the decoration of Deir Mar Mousa were not artists of a high order. But the recovery of the murals is a remarkable achievement that offers compelling visual evidence of the way Christianity continued to flourish in Muslim Syria at the time of the Crusades.

The approach to the monastery.

10. DUMEIR

Some 40 kilometres/25 miles north-east of Damascus, Dumeir is the successor of the Roman Thelsae on the Strata Diocletiana, the key route to Palmyra. The town is skirted by the modern highway. It is a modest enough place, although many buildings were partly constructed with reused masonry from the ancient settlement. But the brief detour is abundantly rewarded by the sight of the handsome Roman temple, which nestles among the crowded domestic buildings. That the level of the modern town is some 5 metres/16 feet above that of the temple helps to explain why this is relatively well preserved. But tactful restoration has also contributed.

An altar of AD 94 now in Paris establishes that a Nabatean temple preceded the existing structure. With three entrances this is unusual in plan and its original function has been the subject of some speculation. The temple is first referred to in connection with a legal suit of 216 and was dedicated to Zeus Hypsistos in 245. The date is significant, as a year earlier the Syrian Philip the Arab had been proclaimed Emperor. The American scholar H.C. Butler, whose archaeological surveys of Syria published between 1903 and 1920 record so much that is now lost, believed that the two portraits in the south pediment of the temple represent Philip and his Empress, Otacilia. But this is far from certain.

The portraits are worn and may never have been of particular refinement. But the masonry itself is of a high order. Characteristic of Romano-Syrian architecture are the angle towers and the internal stairs that led to the roof, which are also found at Palmyra and Isriya.

Like the theatre at Bosra and the Temple of Bel at Palmyra, the temple was adapted as a fortress by the Arabs, rather in the way that Roman arches and other buildings were encased when the Byzantines sought to

The temple: detail.

shore up their faltering control of North Africa. Arab accretions of inferior workmanship survive on the back wall of the temple. The Romans had built their fort some 5 kilometres/3 miles to the east. The walls, with corner towers and central gatehouses, are visible from the main road, near the turn to a military base: the soldiers guarding this are suspicious of cameras and field glasses.

11. THE ROAD TO PALMYRA
Khan al-Manquora, the Harbaqa Dam, Qasr al-Heir al-Gharbi and Khan al-Hallabat

Beyond Dumeir the modern road more or less follows the route of its ancient predecessor, the Strata Diocletiana, north-eastwards to Palmyra. On the left is a chain of hills. To the right the semi-desert stretches to a horizon punctuated by a group of distant outcrops. The prevailing colour is dun or a butterscotch brown; but at times there are patches of white or, where the soil has been disturbed, a poppy red. The road itself can be busy, but as always in the desert one is keenly aware of lateral movement: an angry dog, a small cloud of birds, a lorry driver returning to his vehicle.

Such terrain has always been a challenge to man. And the Romans rose to this. They had to defend their route to Palmyra against marauders and two of their forts illustrate the process. The first, Khan al-Manquora, is below and to the left of the road, about 110 kilometres/68 miles from Damascus. The route descends a broad valley. The fort is placed not far from the northern flank of this, perhaps a kilometre and a half-mile off the modern road, from which it is only visible from the east. An obvious turn-off leads to an isolated farm building: follow tracks to the right of this across a low rise and the khan will be in sight. The walls, four square with towers, are much eroded; but the design is familiar enough, found in variations throughout the Empire from Hadrian's Wall at one extreme to yet more isolated outposts on the eastern frontier. Nothing of note survives within the walls, but to the west of the fort a rectangle of lurid-green vegetation represents its cistern. A line of flourishing plants leading to this marks the course of the channel to which the winter run of a wadi higher up was diverted by a small dam.

The Harbaqa Dam.

The Romans were not pioneers in their use of dams. But they brought to these their remarkable skills of engineering. At al-Buşayri, 40 kilometres/25 miles beyond Khan al-Manquora, turn left for Homs. The road climbs to a higher valley: after 13 kilometres/8 miles, take a track to the left. For a kilometre and a half/1 mile, this follows the margin of the former lake created by the great dam at Harbaqa, across which it turns. The dam, thought to be of the first century AD, is 345 metres/1,130 feet long, some 20 metres/66 feet high at the centre and roughly 18 metres/60 feet thick at the base. It was built of carefully dressed stone filled with rubble, and the calibre of the masonry can still be judged from the downstream, northern wall. Originally channelled northwards by the Romans or their

Palmyrene surrogates, the water from the dam was used in early Arab times for the gardens of the Umayyad lodge of Qasr al-Heir al-Gharbi, the turn for which is on the right, 13 kilometres/8 miles beyond that for Harbaqa.

A line of pylons and buildings on the approach do not seriously compromise the site of the castle. The most impressive extant building is the south half of a substantial tower, originally of four storeys, standing near the corner of the rectangular enclosure. The walls with their semi-circular towers have been largely robbed. The lower courses only survive of the great East Gate, the decorated façade of which is the frontispiece to the Damascus Museum: the use of alternating bands of stone and brick reflected Byzantine example. Outside the gate, a shard bed littered with bricks represents other structures. There is something strangely mesmerizing about such ostensibly insignificant evidence of the

Qasr al-Heir al-Gharbi: bricks and shards in the sand.

past, a scatter of partly consumed bricks and loose stones, strewn in chance patterns across the pale sand. Beyond, the level plain stretches southwards to the chain of low hills that overlook the main roads, ancient and modern, to Palmyra.

Much work has recently been done on the last of the Roman forts on the approach to Palmyra, Khan al-Hallabat, which stands four square in the centre of a valley that is now, once again, fertile. Approximately 31 kilometres/19 miles from Palmyra, the fort can be reached by tracks north of the modern highway. But most visitors will already be excited by the distant streak of green across the ochre prospect, the great oasis to which Palmyra owed its existence, and wish to hurry on to what is by any standard one of the most appealing sites of the ancient world.

12. PALMYRA

Palmyra is with Baalbec and Petra one of the three greatest classical sites of the Near East. No visitor can fail to be struck by the exceptional quality of the monuments of Palmyra's few centuries of high prosperity and moved by the way these seem to grow out of a landscape of inexhaustible beauty. As a child I was fascinated to hear on the Home Service that dust thrown up by the dromedaries on which Queen Zenobia had fled from her city betrayed her to the Romans. But, however dramatic her history, Palmyra owes her existence to nature, or more specifically to the water that falls on the hills to the north and west to feed the oasis that stretches out into the desert. Nowhere else between Damascus and the Euphrates valley could a population of any size be sustained.

Palmyra was settled early in the second millennium BC and the ancient name, Tadmor, is attested in the Bible. The Seleucids, despite their commitment to Dura Europos, seem to have left the inhabitants to themselves. In 41 BC Mark Anthony sought to appropriate their treasure, only to find that the Palmyrenes had withdrawn. The collapse of Seleucid power had already compromised the historic trade route further north and Palmyra was the obvious hub of the alternatives, from the Homs Gap or following the chain of hills from Damascus, which then crossed the desert to the east.

From the reign of Augustus Rome progressively assumed control, and under Nero (54–68) Palmyra became part of the province of Syria. Vying with Antioch, Palmyra was the entrepôt for much of the commerce between the Roman Empire and the east, controlling shipping on the Persian Gulf and importing fabrics from China. In 194 Palmyra became the capital of the new province of Syria Phoenice. Hadrian evidently appreciated the city's cosmopolitan flavour, nominating it a *civitas libera* and endowing it with his name as Palmyra Hadriana. In 212, Caracalla, whose mother Julia Domna came from Emesa (Homs), sought to impose a closer control. Palmyra became a *colonia*. In the ensuing decades the revival of the Sasanians threatened the trading supremacy to which the Palmyrenes had become accustomed. A local family came to prominence and its leader, Septimius Odenathus, was appointed consul and governor of Syria Phoenice in 256–7. He consolidated his position by defending Roman interests after the disaster of 260 at Edessa, when the Emperor Valerian was captured. Odenathus was murdered in 267–8, but his widow, Zenobia, sought to extend Palmyrene power. Bosra was seized and after an Egyptian raid, Zenobia aspired to control Antioch and Anatolia. The new emperor, Aurelian, had no choice but to take her on. Zenobia's retreating army was routed near Emesa in 272. Aurelian then advanced on Palmyra. The captive Zenobia took her part in the Emperor's triumph in Rome two years later. But in the interim the Palmyrenes rose up against the troops Aurelian had left, and it was necessary for him to return. Palmyra was sacked. The treasure of the Temple of Bel was appropriated, and the city became a garrison town, which was walled under Diocletian in face of the Persian threat.

Under the Byzantines the population evidently shrank, although the Emperor Justinian restored the walls. Palmyra fell to the Arabs in 634. The city walls were torn down after a rebellion in 745 and the place gradually declined. Yet its continuing strategic value is implied by the twelfth-century fortification of the Temple of Bel and the more or less contemporary construction of Qalaat Ibn Maan on the commanding hill to the west. Material for both projects was inevitably quarried from the ruins, but the absence of a settled population means that these were thereafter left to wind and time.

The remains at Tadmor were known to Western merchants based at Aleppo long before they were systematically recorded by the Torinese architect Giovanni Battista Borra for Wood and Dawkins in 1751. It was at Palmyra that William Pitt's niece, Lady Hester Stanhope, was acclaimed, at least to her own satisfaction, as Queen of the Desert. Now Palmyra is inexorably on the tourist trail. And although great efforts have been made to concentrate development in the new town, one can only regret the unsympathetic recent extension to the pre-war Zenobia Hotel, which overlooks the site, and the even larger complexes that now compete with the unappealing Cham Palace Hotel on the southern approach.

The old main road that sweeps across the site affords a classic *coup d'oeil* of the ruins, with the decumanus stretching to the west and the Sanctuary of Bel on the right, backed by the fierce greens of small orchards, confined behind blank walls of mud. The tourist's priorities must depend on the hour of arrival and the length of time at his disposal. The great Temple of Bel is rewarding in any light, but I shall never forget my first visit by moonlight in 1993 – since when, alas, the gap in the temenos wall to which it was then possible to climb has been filled in. The museum provides a welcome refuge from the midday sun, and it is there that one must arrange to visit the best-preserved tombs. The colonnaded street is at its most magical in the late afternoon, when it is equally rewarding to walk on among the clusters of tower tombs and up to the castle. Every pebble is caught in the sinking sunlight. But don't linger when the buses disgorge their passengers. Try to be at the top of Diocletian's fort when the sun at length sinks.

Most visitors arrive in the late morning, so there is a case for starting at the museum. This is somewhat run down. But there is no better place to orientate oneself. The collection of Palmyrene sculpture is unrivalled. This reflects both classical and Parthian influence. Some of the finest things are in the third room: an admirably crisp statue of a youth, a representation of a man in Persian costume and a relief of a sailing boat, which reminds us of the tentacles of the Palmyrene economy. The portrait tradition that developed at Palmyra was clearly conditioned by the expectations of Palmyra's mercantile ruling class. The

Palmyrene portrait, outside the museum.

sculptors knew well that their patrons had a keen interest in the fabrics they wore and with which they draped their furniture. Certain physical types recur. Thus the beautiful relief of Aqna, daughter of Ateline, in the central hall is emphatically Semitic. Other portraits anticipate Byzantine and even Pisan sculpture, while the elderly man with a knitted brow could have lived in any society. The smaller finds enrich our understanding of a very distant world.

The temple of Bel, with capitals originally sheathed in metal and the oasis beyond.

From the museum, follow the fringe of the oasis to the Temple of Bel, which, as Burns fairly states, is 'the most important religious building of the 1st Century AD in the Middle East'. The great square of the peribolos walls stands on a high terrace. This dates from 80–120 AD, but the former propylaeum, the ceremonial gate, on the west front was completed only at the end of the second century. This was demolished a millennium later when the walls were fortified. The modern ticket office is to the left of the rebuilt section, and one emerges just to the right of the original sunken sacrificial entrance.

Ahead, not placed centrally but set back to the east on a high podium, is the cella. This was dedicated in 32 AD, and took the place of a shrine that had already been established for over two thousand years. The temple is a subtle fusion of Semitic and classical traditions. The oblong cella is set within a peristyle, eight immensely tall Corinthian columns of which stand on the east side: the roughly blocked-out capitals were originally sheathed in metal. A broad flight of steps precedes the entrance, which also is not centrally placed. The elaborately decorated door-case was restored in 1932. Near this are the surviving limestone beams that joined the cornice above the peristyle to the cella walls, with sharply cut reliefs of local deities. At either end of the cella are shrines, or adytons. Bel is represented on the lintel of the north adyton, which has a well-preserved ceiling. A stair to the left of this leads to the roof, which had an important role in religious observances, but as the original steps up to the adyton have been lost and concrete has been used to eliminate handholds, this is now not easily reached. The southern adyton, nearer the door, is smaller but equally elaborate. Through the medium of Wood and Dawkins's publication the remarkable carved ceiling was much admired in Georgian England.

Descending from the cella, one cannot but be awed by the space within the peribolos. While there was only a single arcade on the west side, elsewhere there were double rows of columns, of which that to the south is the best preserved. Wandering around, it is not difficult to see where the walls were renewed by the Arabs and have subsequently been restored. The fall of light on the columns and walls seems to change at every step, and the undulating drama of the hills is unforgettable.

To the east of the temple are the orchards. Lanes meander between mud walls, and even in the heat of the day there is shade. That is most emphatically no longer to be found on the colonnaded decumanus, 1.2 kilometres/three-quarters of a mile long, which is perhaps the most familiar sight of Palmyra. This was unpaved – to spare camels' hoofs – and although construction was begun from the further end, it is more practical to explore it in reverse. The easternmost section is largely lost. Just across the modern road a monumental arch masks a thirty-degree change of direction in a masterly way. This was built under Septimius Severus (193–211). A number of key public buildings were off the next stretch

of the street and may indeed have in part dictated its alignment: the now fragmentary Temple of Nebo and the excessively restored theatre. Behind the latter is an altogether more satisfying group of buildings, including the Tarrif Court and the enclosed agora. But for most visitors it is the street itself that holds the attention, and the long if incomplete rows of columns with brackets on which statues were originally placed that haunt the imagination.

The reconstructed tetrapylon masks a second but less dramatic change in direction: only one of the columns of pink Egyptian granite is original. A side road to the right leads to the Temple of Baal-Shamin, begun in AD 17. The cella of AD 130, picturesquely overgrown with trees, is unexpectedly exuberant in taste, with a beautiful small exedra. To the west of the road are the foundations of a group of Byzantine churches, and the peristyles of a number of mansions poke up above the pale soil. These repay attention, but most visitors will want to walk on up the decumanus, towards the handsome funerary temple that marks its western end. Here one is particularly aware of the way nearly two centuries of wind-blown sand have eaten into the stone: a deliquescent Corinthian capital here, the eroded stump of a column there. The temple itself has been restored with considerable tact, using concrete where the original blocks were lost. The carving of the pilasters with entwined vines and with acanthus is most satisfying. So too, as I lingered, was the mingling of the muezzin's call with the sounds of children from the farm near by, playing with a ball.

In front of the temple was the intersection of the decumanus with a second colonnaded street that ran southwards to the small oval forum just within the Damascus Gate. Above this, to the west, approached by a further colonnaded road, was the principia of the camp, built between 293 and 303 by Sosianus Hierocles, governor of Syria under Diocletian. The wall of the fort ran up the steep hill behind the principia, and it is

The Temple of Bel: north-west corner of the temenos.

from this vantage point that Palmyra can best be watched at sunset. The ruins are gilded in the low light and then begin to disappear in shadow as the last of the sun illuminates the oasis and the pale desert beyond.

The main necropolis stretches for roughly a kilometre/half a mile on either side of the valley to the south-west of the Damascus Gate. The cluster of tower tombs on the oval hill across the wadi, Umm al-Belqis, is one of the most haunting sights of Palmyra. Another group is on the flank of the Jebel Husseiniye. Further on there is a larger concentration of towers. The best preserved is the Tomb of Elahbel. This was built in AD 103 for four brothers. There were spaces for no fewer than 300 bodies, on four levels above a hypogeum. The main entrance is on the south and opens to a lavishly decorated passage. This retains most of the vault with reliefs of heads and much original pigmentation. Visits can be arranged at the museum and also take in the second-century Hypogeum of the Three Brothers in the south-west necropolis, off the Damascus road. Steps lead down to the tomb, the large central chamber within which is flanked by smaller lateral extensions. Much of the sculpture is intact, but the hypogeum is more remarkable for the murals. On the end wall the brothers themselves are depicted in roundels borne by genii. The details of the *trompe l'oeil* architecture are beautifully rendered and the animals are well observed. The keyholder, for a consideration, may be prepared to take you to the Tomb of Arteban in the south-east necropolis on the fringe of the oasis. This first-century hypogeum was found accidentally in 1958: the sculpture is of consistently refined quality.

The Qalaat Ibn Maan which hangs over the city was formerly regarded as the work of Fakhr al-Din (1590–1635), whose challenge to Ottoman authority led to his execution. But recent restoration work has shown that this incorporates much of the fabric of a medieval castle that was evidently contemporary with the fortification of the Temple of Bel.

The colonnaded street, with Qalaat Ibn Maan beyond.

The castle attracts huge mobs at sunset. Few tourists, however, trouble with one of the most evocative sites of classical Syria, the quarries some 10 kilometres/6 miles to the north-east of Palmyra. A road from the northern bypass heads to a 'collection point' below the escarpment: a track to the right curls up to higher ground, from which ancient excavations are visible on a low ridge ahead. The herringbone cuttings are sharpest where they have been protected from the prevailing west wind. A stack of rough-hewn columns awaits collection. Where labourers once worked, there is an eerie silence. Red poppies wave in the wind and the eye is drawn to the Qalaat Ibn Maan in the distance.

The quarries.

13. QASR AL-HEIR AL-SHARQI

In a memorable passage of his *Syria*, Robin Fedden recorded his excitement on the approach to Qasr al-Heir al-Sharqi, the great Umayyad 'palace' in semi-desert some 140 kilometres/87 miles east of Palmyra. On my first visit, when dust kicked up by the First Gulf War hung as a pall of grey cloud to the east, I found a guide at Sukne who used only two words of English, 'one' and 'two', to indicate the gears he considered I ought to select. We followed tracks across the level sand, keeping to the south of low hills until the two fortresses stood out in the distance below the wide horizon. But now, at least for those without four-wheel drive, it is much simpler to take the metalled road north from Sukne and turn eastwards at Taybah, once the Roman fort of Oriza, where a fallen column lies beside a handsome minaret, itself built of reused blocks.

Qasr al-Heir was well placed to monitor traffic between Palmyra and the Euphrates, and the site was first occupied by the Palmyrenes. But the two fortified enclosures, the larger to the west, and the minaret with the foundations of the associated mosque between these, were willed into existence by the Caliph Hisham (724–45). Settlement on the scale implied was made possible by a dam on higher ground 30 kilometres/19 miles to the north-west. The water from this was fed to a huge demesne, about 850 hectares/2,100 acres in extent and enclosed by a 22-kilometre/14-mile circuit of mud-brick walls, traces of which can be recognized. Intensely cultivated, this must have required a substantial workforce. The notion that it was a vast garden, however, seems far-fetched, although such flowers as red tulips are still to be found in the vicinity.

Both the fortresses are square in plan, and built in a distinctive grey sandstone. The eastern castle is the better preserved, but its impact is

Qasr al-Heir al-Sharqi.

now somewhat marred by the colour of the material used in the recent restoration. There are round towers at the corners and two semi-circular ones on each side, those to the west placed close together flanking the gate. This is surmounted by a relieving arch of a type long used in Syria, on which traces of early painted decoration can be seen. Brick is employed to visual effect in the frieze, perhaps echoing Mesopotamian sources, although the Byzantines had of course relished the contrast of stone and brick: and the machicolation above the gate is an early example of the use of that most effective defensive device. The building may have been intended as a khan. There was a central courtyard with a colonnade of recycled columns, some of which were fluted, presumably brought from Palmyra or one of the Roman forts in the area. Around this were a series of high rooms with brick barrel vaults: some of these are in place, although most have collapsed.

Between the two enclosures is the elegant minaret. This can still be climbed, but care must be taken in the upper two sections, the steps of which have fallen. There is no better vantage point from which to survey the ruins. Recent excavations have revealed the foundations of the associated mosque.

The western enceinte was defended by twenty-eight towers. Four of the five gates were aligned on streets that led to a large central piazza, once porticoed. At the south-eastern corner is the most convincingly palatial structure at Qasr al-Heir, with excellent columns of grey marble, which has recently been cleared. On the fall of the Umayyads, Syria passed to the Abbasids, who seem to have maintained Qasr al-Heir until the tenth century. The place was apparently reoccupied a century later, only to be abandoned in the wake of the Mongol depredations. Now there is a settlement at a tactful distance. The guardian can see any car that arrives from his house and leap on to his motorcycle with the keys, so it is no longer necessary to climb into the smaller castle.

14. DEIR AL-ZOR

Deir al-Zor on the right bank of the Euphrates has no monuments to commend it. As the point where the main roads from Aleppo to Baghdad and from Damascus to the Jezira cross, the town has an obvious strategic importance. But Burnet Pavitt, my erstwhile neighbour, who spent a period in charge of its civil administration during the Second World War, could recall only one memorable experience there: de Gaulle's indignation at learning that an Englishman should hold the post.

For obvious geographical reasons Deir al-Zor is the best base from which to visit sites on the mid-Euphrates, including Dura Europos, Mari and Halebiye; and the relatively modern Archaeological Museum at the northern end of the town deserves to be better known.

The museum is arranged chronologically, and by using reconstructions and casts from works kept elsewhere, as well as original items, offers a compelling microcosm of the archaeology of the Euphrates valley and of the Jezira, the great plain between the river and the Tigris where numerous tells attest to early occupation. Thus the finds of c.6400–5900 BC from Tell Bouqra, south of the town, are shown in cases set into a reconstruction of a mud-brick house. There are bone tools and arrowheads of flint and obsidian. The pottery is of considerable refinement and the clay models include a small male head and a seated woman with pendulous breasts. Particularly fine are some of the animals: a tortoise in pumice, an alabaster hare and vases in the same medium in the forms of a hedgehog and a bull.

Other sites are represented: Tell Brak, with eye idols datable to 3500–3300 BC and animal figurines, as well as a substantial limestone bull with a human head and neatly furled legs, and rather later (1450–1300 BC) so-called Nuzi ware, with decorative designs including stylized cranes; and

Tell Mozan, with a terracotta goat of c.2400 BC. Particularly interesting in view of later architectural developments is the reconstruction of the mud-brick gateway at Tell Bderi, of about 2700 BC. The gate is flanked by orthostats, or slabs of stone; below each of the towers at either side there is a glacis.

From the first millennium BC are neo-Hittite reliefs of winged bulls and of genii found at Tell Ajaja. The poorly preserved mural of a garden from Tell Sheikh Hamad, of the seventh century BC, offers early visual evidence of the fascination gardens held for so many civilizations of the Near East.

There are fewer exhibits of the classical period. Yet these hint at the way competing powers and patterns of trade overlapped in the Euphrates valley. Thus there is a wide cultural gap between the small relief of a splendidly dressed Parthian man from Dura and the Roman statue, variously identified as an emperor or Mars, placed near by, while the fragments of silk from a tomb at Halebiye must have been imported from China. The panorama continues with elaborate window frames and fragments of friezes in stucco of AD 727 from Qasr al-Heir al-Sharqi, ending on an unexpected note with a bicycle tied to an early street lamp.

As the museum hints, Deir al-Zor is the obvious starting place for a circuit of the Jezira, watered by the Khabur, which meets the Euphrates some 45 kilometres/28 miles to the south, near the dusty tell of the town's Roman predecessor, Circessium. The valley of the Khabur is marked by a sequence of tells, mute witnesses of a past of which we gradually learn more from archaeology. On the left bank, some 60 kilometres/37 miles from Deir al-Zor, is Tell Sheikh Hamid, the Assyrian Dur Katlimu, where some eroded excavations can be seen. The main concentration of excavated tells is further north, in a triangle formed by the Khabur and the Jaghiagh, which flows into it at Haseke. The sites of most interest to the non-specialist are Tell Halaf on the river Khabur by the Turkish frontier west of Ras al-Ain, where Baron von Oppenheim excavated the sculptures now in Berlin and at Aleppo; Tell Mozan, to the west of Al-Qamishli; and Tell Brak, a vast mound by the Jaghiagh first worked on by Sir Max Mallowan. Some 35 kilometres/22 miles north of Haseke is Tell Beydar, where an impressive palace complex of about 2400 BC has been responsibly conserved. Distance and inadequate hotels exclude the Jezira from most itineraries, but the bare landscape from which tells rise in almost bewildering number has a poignant beauty.

15. QALAAT RAHBA

Some castles are memorable because they are well preserved – Krak des Chevaliers is of course a prime example. Others owe their magic to their deliquescence. So it is with sand and wind-eroded Rahba, which is an unforgettable memory, bathed in the glowing light of late afternoon, on the return northwards from Dura Europos.

All rulers of Syria have sought to control the Euphrates. Nur al-Din (1146–74) was no exception. The construction of Rahba was supervised by an officer in his service, Malik Ibn Tauk. Its position, on a rise near the river, had already been selected by the Abbasids, and material from their fortress was no doubt incorporated in the new structure. Like other Syrian fortresses of the period, Rahba was defended by a substantial moat. But it was very different in layout from the castles higher up the Euphrates valley, Jaber and Najim. The pentagonal walls surround a central motte, topped by a keep, which is also a pentagon in plan. Those who like to clamber on shattered masonry or venture into gloomy substructures will not be disappointed, and the enormous cistern cannot fail to impress.

In the shifting political world of medieval Syria, Rahba may only have had a relatively brief importance, although as late as 1264 a governor of the castle was appointed by the great Mameluke sultan, Baibars, whose territorial ambition was directed towards Mesopotamia rather than to the reduction of Crusader fortresses in the west. Now the castle has another function, as a place of recreation for the local youth: adolescents may want to practise their English, while their fearless younger brothers climb the time-scarred walls.

The castle at dusk.

16. DURA EUROPOS

There has been much recent development in the Euphrates valley, the right bank of which is fringed by minor towns. But the context of the ruins of Dura Europos has happily been respected. The road rises to a bare plain and 93 kilometres/58 miles south of Deir al-Zor the walls come into view on the left. Although partly silted up by sand, these remain immensely impressive and imply the importance of the city.

Founded early in the third century BC by Nicanor, a general who served Seleucus I Nicator, who himself had been born at Europos in Macedonia, the city was laid out on a grid plan. Probably in 113 BC effective control passed from the Seleucids to the Parthians, for whom Dura with its Macedonian and Semitic inhabitants became the entrepôt of the western flank of their empire. The Romans, who built their own forward post of Circesium on the left bank of the river, did not challenge Parthia's rule at Dura until AD 115, when Trajan took it. His heir, Hadrian, returned Dura to the Parthians, but in 164 it was recovered for Rome, to be nominated a colony in 211. After 224 increasing tensions with the Parthians, Sasanian successors led to much Roman military activity at Dura, where rival religious communities – pagan, Christian and Jewish – coexisted, underpinning the city's commercial domination of the Middle Euphrates. This was challenged by the Sasanians and, despite Roman endeavours to repair the walls, Shapur took the city in a hard-fought siege of 256. He sacked it. Dura never recovered. But as a result the evidence of its Parthian and Roman phases was not obliterated by subsequent occupation. Protected by the encroaching sand, Dura was fortunate not to attract further attention until the age of scientific excavation in the interwar years.

The Seleucids chose a position that lent itself perfectly to their purposes, protected to the north-east by the river and at either side by deep wadis. Only to the south-west was the site vulnerable; and here the Seleucids laid out the massive walls that must have always offered anyone who did not arrive from the river his first impression of the place. Originally partly built of mud brick, but with stone towers, the walls were probably reinforced by the Parthians in the first century AD.

Enter by the Great, or Palmyra, Gate, as massive as its name suggests. During the siege of 256, the Romans sought to counteract the danger of the Sasanians' mining the walls by piling massive quantities of sand against them. It is to this that the survival of the synagogue – with the murals now at Damascus – is due: it was just beyond the first tower to the north of the gate. The excavators learnt something of the horror of the siege when they found the bones of the soldiers buried when a Sasanian mine and a Roman counter mine collapsed under the tower immediately to the north.

On entering the town it might seem logical to follow the cardo, which is flanked in the centre of the town by the agora on the left and three temples on the right. But as these are reduced to little more than foundations, it is visually more rewarding to follow the walls to the right, past what remains of the chapel of AD 232. Above the wadi to the south the walls follow the contour of the ground, with massive bastions at exposed salients. The original configuration is at places obscured by excavation spoil. As the ground falls away towards the Euphrates there are beautiful views to the river. Near the south-eastern corner of the town are the substantial ruins of the House of Lysias, with a generous peristyle. Beyond is the early citadel, the north wall of which has been restored, above a deep valley that cuts into the town. In the fold of this is a recently reconstructed Roman house.

Much more impressive is the south-western wall of the Seleucid citadel, 300 metres/328 yards long, with three massive towers. There are three entrances. Within, although there is clear evidence as to where internal

buildings abutted on the wall, little survives. The eastern walls have long since been consumed, for the Euphrates has been insatiable, gnawing hungrily away at the partly undercut cliffs. A bird of prey glides on the thermals and the sounds of a motor boat and a pump rise from the river. Venture as near the edge of the cliff as is safe to look down at the Euphrates, a pale blue under the sand-laden December mist, a stronger blue in the more generous spring. Below is a low island, which no doubt developed after a cliff fall. Across the great river, the level landscape of the Jezira stretches to an infinite horizon.

Emerging from the western gate of the citadel, one can climb up the side of the wadi to regain the city wall as it curves round the flank of the valley to the north. You come to the arches of an aqueduct, associated with a bath complex to the south; beyond it are the scant remains of the amphitheatre. Further on, just inside the wall, is the praetorium of the Roman camp. The Temple of the Palmyrene Gods, with the reconstructed stumps of four columns, and the Temple of Mithras were built against the wall, the second just before the point where this turns to run in a straight line to the Great Gate. As the light sinks it is oddly satisfying to make across the town for the agora, and then to leave Dura, as it should be left, by the Great Gate. But if there is time before leaving, examine the outer face of the wall, with its measured bastions and marvellously disciplined masonry.

Tower mined in AD 256.

17. MARI

Mari, on the right bank of the Euphrates, may have been founded in the early fourth millennium BC, but it only became a major Sumerian city in the Early Dynastic period (2900–2300 BC). Although subject to the Akkadian Empire from 2340 BC until this fell in about 2150 BC, Mari became a considerable trading centre, mediating between the city states of Mesopotamia and her rivals to the north and west. Its rulers, the Amorites, were Semitic. Mari's increasing wealth must have been seen as a challenge by her neighbours and no doubt led to the suppression of the dynasty by Shamsi-Adad of Assyria in about 1800 BC. After his death the Amorite King Zimri-Lim regained control. But once again the evident prosperity of Mari had a political price: the city was conquered in 1759 BC by a rival Amorite king who aspired to rule Mesopotamia, Hammurabi of Babylon, whose laws are inscribed in such uncompromising terms on the celebrated stela now in the Louvre. Two years later he destroyed the town walls and temples; and the tell was effectively abandoned until the invasion of the archaeologists in the interwar years.

Significantly the builders of Mari did not feel the need of an elevated defensive site like that of Dura Europos, only 25 kilometres/15 miles to the north: the tell, although unusual in extent, is not conspicuous in height. And the visitor who has not seen the remarkable statues from the site in the Louvre and at Damascus, or read about the extraordinary archive Mari yielded, may wonder why he or she should contend with a great hump of impacted mud, which, in areas where the excavator's spoil is in view, takes on the character of a moonscape.

For the non-archaeologist there is no point in trying to analyse too exactly the various excavations. Almost all of these have suffered as a result of half a century's exposure to rain and wind. It is enough to know that the Great Palace completed by King Zimri-Lim, which was the nerve centre of his realm, boasted 272 rooms and that there were fanes to Ishtar and other, less familiar, local deities, Ninni-Zaza, Shamash and Dagan. While there are small sections of well-preserved mud-brick walls across the site, it is only in the covered section of the palace that the casual visitor is offered any sense of the architectural ambition of the rulers of Mari. Narrow rooms and passages open off a courtyard, in which some of the decorative elements of the mud structure survive. There is of course no trace of the murals for which Mari is so famous, or of the colour that her rulers would have expected. But they would still recognize the timeless quality of the view to the east, where the Euphrates is fringed by the pale brown earth and by the almost lurid greens of the crops and trees which it nurtures.

The Great Palace of Zimri-Lim, mud brick emerging from the tell.

18. BAGHUZ

Were it not hardly 15 kilometres/9 miles from Mari, Baghuz, near the site of Corsoteh, a city recorded by Xenophon and itself the successor of the earlier Nagiateh, might have no claim on the tourist. The changing course of the Euphrates may explain why the city proper has left no trace. The visitor should cross the river by the bridge 4 kilometres/2½ miles north of the centre of the border town of Abu Kemal, and then turn right towards the escarpment on the further side of the level valley.

Although this is overtopped by a water tower, it is easy to see the most accessible of the tower tombs. Some half a kilometre/one third of a mile north of the point where the cliff was spectacularly cut away by the river in the past, it is set on a slight knob. The north face is decorated with pilasters. Steps rise in successive stages to the roof; the funerary chamber itself was below the tower. A further tomb can be seen to the south, set back from the cliff; others can be found by following the road that runs below the ridge northwards, crossing to a track that skirts a graveyard, to turn by a makeshift football pitch. There are the stumps of two towers and footings of others, all placed on the crest of the rise for effect, marking as it were the frontier between the desert and the town, for one looks down from the windswept escarpment to the prosperous villages below with their ordered fields.

The tombs resemble their Palmyrene counterparts and were presumably constructed between the first and third centuries for prominent families of the Parthian town that guarded the Euphrates. The river then divided the empire of Iran from that of Rome. Baghuz now, once again, is near a frontier that has to be closely watched. I took some time to realize that the two men who directed me to the right tracks were from the mukhabarat (secret police). Being shadowed in so helpful a way was

Tower tomb.

unexpectedly reassuring, and did not diminish the appeal of the place. For ruinous as these are, the wind-torn monuments of Baghuz are oddly moving.

19. HALEBIYE AND ZALEBIYE

Control of the Euphrates was vital to the defence of Syria, and the prodigious fortress of Halebiye shows how high a priority this represented for the Byzantines under the Emperor Justinian (527–65). Some 46 kilometres/29 miles north of Deir al-Zor, the modern road up the right bank of the river meets a range of hills, the al-Khanuqa, 'the strangler', which closes in upon the river. A side road to the right follows the escarpment. Immediately the tempo changes: a boy and his sister ride on a donkey; a pack of five dogs rush up to the road. In the villages there are piles of brushwood. On the slope above the river are a number of encampments, with lorries drawn up around the tents, long lines hung with washing and large flocks of sheep. Ahead, through the morning mist, is the prodigious southern wall of Halebiye, suspended from the detached hill of the citadel and running down to the water's edge.

The position was well chosen. It was fortified in the third century by the Palmyrenes, doubtless under Zenobia, whose name it was given. Later it was reinforced when Diocletian sought to protect Syria from Rome's Persian enemies. Their successors, the Sasanians, were formidable foes in Justinian's time, and the Emperor, who had done so much to restore Byzantine fortunes elsewhere, understood the importance of defending his Syrian flank. Birtha, as Halebiye was then known, is the ultimate expression of his policy. It was designed by two architects – one of whom was a nephew of Isidorus of Miletus, who rebuilt Haghia Sophia at Constantinople – and executed to the highest specifications. Birtha must have strained the imperial coffers; and the maintenance of this and other Byzantine fortresses meant that the indigenous population had to be heavily taxed. Like all the strongholds of Byzantine Syria, Birtha – and its lesser counterpart of Zalebiye – fell to the Arabs after the Battle of the

Halebiye: the southern wall and the citadel.

Yarmuk in 636. No longer of strategic significance, Halebiye, the citadel apart, was abandoned. Happily the fabric was spared from predators because the region was sparsely inhabited until relatively recent times.

The walls defend a triangular area of some 12 hectares/30 acres. The modern road enters by the South Gate, near the south-east corner, and more or less follows the line of the main street. The south wall, with ten towers in addition to those of the gatehouse, is some 550 metres/1,800 feet in length. The rather shorter wall above the river is less spectacular. The provision of three gates in this, however, suggests how important access to the river was to Birtha's prosperity as a trading post.

The northern wall is particularly impressive. Start at the north gate and follow the line upwards. There are four substantial square towers of Justinian's time, consistent in plan: passages on the upper level reached by flights of stairs link these. Careful thought was clearly given to ensuring the best possible sight lines for archers, and the masonry is consistently of the highest quality: many of the calcareous gypsum blocks are as crisp as when they were quarried.

Beyond the fourth tower, on more steeply rising ground, is the praetorium. The detail is similar to that of the towers, but here there are three storeys rather than two. Brick was used for the vaulting and, despite earthquake damage, the whole is sufficiently well preserved for one to be able to take in much of the internal arrangements.

Above the praetorium is the citadel. This was altered in Arab times, and is most remarkable for its position. The defender could have monitored any movement from either direction along the river, or from the higher ground to the west. On the descent, look down across the site. At your feet is the West Church, with a large apse, also Justinian in date, to the left of which is a small room with a basin. Below this, and to the right, is a smaller, earlier church, which originally was richly decorated, as a fluted column drum and fragments of a Corinthian capital indicate. Near by are vestiges of the forum.

The tower tombs of Halebiye were associated with the Palmyrene settlement. The lower section of one stands prominently above the road to the south, but the main necropolis was to the north. There is a cluster of eroded husks opposite the walls and further on nearer the road a less fragmentary group. Beyond these a better-preserved tower stands higher up the slope. This retains some of its original stucco decoration, with pilasters and false windows, particularly on the north where it was protected from the sun; the chamber within is domed. The necropolis was maintained in Roman times, as a handful of rock-cut tombs indicate.

Were it not for the proximity of its greater counterpart, Zalebiye would rank as one of the more remarkable Byzantine fortresses in Syria. The construction of a pontoon bridge across the Euphrates, a few hundred metres north of Halebiye, means that it is no longer necessary to make a

Zalebiye, with the Euphrates below.

massive detour up the left bank of the Euphrates to reach Zalebiye. Cross the bridge, turn south and take a track to the right of the ramp to the bridge over the railway and then continue: Zalebiye is ahead.

The fortress we see was built under Justinian to complement the larger stronghold of Halebiye and thus to secure control of the Euphrates. But the site had already been occupied by the Palmyrenes for similar strategic reasons. The bluff, high above the river, was roughly rectangular, but has now been partly consumed by the river. What survives is the greater part of the east wall of the fortress, approached up a steep slope. Here, as at Halebiye, the builders used beautifully cut calcareous stone. The fine gateway is similar to those of Halebiye and relatively well preserved. To the left the wall is reinforced by three towers. The nearer is much shattered, but the interior arrangements of the one beyond and of that at the south-east angle can still be understood. The southern wall was less well defended by the fall of the ground and its western section has been swept away by the Euphrates. Within the fortress a few buildings can be partly traced. The north-eastern angle of the wall is now in immediate danger. There are fissures in the outcrop and exposed blocks hang above the abyss, waiting to join others that have already fallen. Two fishermen in the rowing boat below have, however, no exaggerated sense of danger. The river is, nonetheless, eating away at the site. On the slope below the main gate there is abundant evidence of a settlement that must have depended on the fortress, with scatterings of basalt fragments and of shards.

20. RAQQA

Raqqa, on the left bank of the Euphrates, seems originally to have been named after Seleucus II Callinicos, c.244 BC, and was occupied by the Romans and Byzantines, whose heroic general Belisarius failed to stem a Persian assault near by in 531. The last great Umayyad, Caliph Hisham, constructed two palaces at Raqqa. Late in his successful reign (754–75), the Abbasid Caliph al-Mansur, who had already built a new capital at Baghdad, selected Raqqa as his secondary capital and the administrative centre of the Jezira – the territory between the Euphrates and the Tigris. Al-Mansur's Baghdad was circular in plan, but here the position of the river meant that while the northern half of the walls was also laid out on a circular scheme, the southern section was built as if on a rectangle. Raqqa would remain a place of importance until the Mongols sacked it in 1258. Only in the last century did its population recover; the ancient town is now at the heart of a substantial conurbation.

Raqqa makes no concession to the tourist. The great horseshoe of brick walls, so atmospherically described by Fedden and appealing in early photographs, has been vigorously rebuilt. Only in the odd place where the new skin of brick has disintegrated can the original structure be seen. There were originally over a hundred round towers. The one spectacular gate is the heavily restored Bab Baghdad at the south-east corner, which is surmounted by a row of blind arches in intricate patterns: this is now dated to the twelfth century.

Al-Mansur placed his Great Mosque, begun in 772, near the centre of his city. The complex was square, the outer wall with eleven towers of which the lower sections have been reconstructed. What remains is attributable to Nur al-Din's reconstruction of 1165–6: an austere tower and, across the former courtyard from this, the arcade of the prayer hall, with beautifully articulated modulations in the design of the outer arches and a large inscription above the central opening. Decorative stucco from the mosque, as well as fragments of a tiled inscription and metalwork, are in the uncompromisingly old-fashioned museum near the modern souk. Within the walls, south of the main eastern entrance, is the restored hulk of the ninth-century Qasr al-Banat (Palace of the Maidens), with at its centre a courtyard flanked by four iwans, which reveal the influence of contemporary Persian architecture.

Raqqa falls rather between two stools. It is not sufficiently well preserved to have high priority on a sightseeing circuit; and what it does have to offer is visually strangled by the living town. But the hotel is not as dire as accounts suggest and Raqqa can be a useful place to stay, as there is much to see between Deir al-Zor and Aleppo.

The Great Mosque.

21. RESAFE

Few ruins are more poignant than Resafe. The near rectangle of the great walls reconstructed for the Emperor Justinian seems still to defy the level expanses of the semi-desert. The site had been occupied much earlier and was first fortified under Diocletian (284–305), for whom it was of importance both as the junction of two major Roman roads that converged to cross the Euphrates at Sura and as a key post on the Strata Diocletiana which followed the route south to Palmyra and beyond. But it was to another of Diocletian's campaigns that Resafe's later distinction was due. In the last year of his reign, before retiring to Spalato on the Dalmatian coast, Diocletian unleashed an energetic persecution of the Christians. A soldier called Sergius was martyred at Resafe. He came to be widely revered; and under Anastasius I (491–515) a large basilica was built and the town, which had clearly become a major pilgrimage centre, was renamed Sergiopolis.

Justinian's now sand-scarred gypsum walls replaced Anastasius's circuit of mud brick. Reinforced by numerous towers, both square and round, these survive for the most part to full height. The remarkable North Gate was clearly intended as a Christian counterpart to the processional entrances to the temenoi of earlier temples. But the Emperor's engineers built also for defence. A relatively modest entrance through a projecting outer wall opened to an enclosed court dominated by the richly decorated triple inner gateway.

The scale of the area within the walls always comes as a surprise. On a first visit it makes sense to follow the line of the road that crossed the town to the South Gate, now blocked. The first building of interest, to

Passageway in the north wall.

The Church of St Sergius: capital.

the left, is a much-ruined church. Datable to the 520s, this was particularly ingenious in the way a central circular space was contrived within the traditional basilica plan. This elegance in plan was matched by the quality of the masonry. Some of the columns were of a yellow marble and there are traces of red paint in the fluting of others. Beyond, also on the left, is the relatively modest Byzantine market building, so similar in layout to ottoman khans built over a millennium later.

A hundred metres/109 yards or so further on – to the right – is the first of three huge Byzantine barrel-vaulted cisterns. The historian Procopius believed that these were built for Justinian, but they are now thought to be of earlier date. Even by the standard of the great cisterns of Constantinople those of Resafe are remarkable. The largest, in two sections, is to the south and had a capacity of some 15,000 cubic metres/19,600 cubic yards. The cisterns provided the lifeblood of Sergiopolis, for without these it would have been impossible to sustain a substantial population in the face of drought or prolonged siege. It is no longer possible to go down the dusty stair to the bottom of the main cistern, and care should be taken when looking down through the openings on the end walls.

Some way to the east, behind the market, is the church known as Basilica B, which may have been the centre of the cult of St Sergius, before the much larger church ahead was constructed. The addition of a fourth aisle on the south side proves that in its day Basilica B was a pilgrimage centre of some importance.

The great church now associated with St Sergius was originally dedicated in 559 to the Holy Cross. The central nave was divided from the side aisles on each side by three huge arches supported on elegant cruciform piers, a variant on the scheme already adopted at Qalb Lozeh. But although the arches were only intended to carry a wooden roof, within twenty years it proved necessary to underpin them with pairs of smaller arches resting on yellowish columns. Stability was thus achieved, but at the cost of losing what must have been an innovative sense of interlocking space. In its roofless state we do not immediately sense how dark the church must have been, with light filtered through the rows of small windows above the lateral arches. But the refinement of the construction can still be read in the inscribed capitals and in such details as the cornice. Some traces of original stucco still adhere to the masonry.

The basilica is not far from the eastern wall and for those with time it is certainly worth following this from the south-eastern angle. The East Gate, although of some pretension, is notably less ambitious than its northern counterpart. Perhaps the finest stretch of the wall is on the north. Here one can follow a long section of the open passage that gave access to the towers, or mount to the upper walkway. From this vantage point the extant buildings, remarkable as they are, seem almost insignificant as they rise above the undulating soil to which time and treasure hunters have reduced the city. Here, particularly when the sun is low, we are reminded of Poidebard's aerial photograph of 1934, which no doubt inspired the composer Charlie Usher's recent *Resafe from the Air*. In 1934 Resafe stood in glorious isolation. Now a tarmac road follows the walls and there is a scattering of modern houses in the middle distance. But the most striking building that can be seen from the walls is a few hundred metres from the north gate: the gypsum hulk of a palace with domed chambers that may have been occupied by one of the Ghassanids. Three kilometres/2 miles to the south, on the line of the Roman road, is a small outpost, again of gypsum, with barrel-vaulted rooms.

Justinian's Resafe was to be relatively short lived. His successors were unable to deter their long-standing Persian adversary. Chosroes II sacked Resafe in 616 and with the Arab victory of 636 the fortress became an irrelevance. A century later the last of the great Umayyads, the Caliph Hisham (724–43), recognized the potential of the place and must have used the Byzantine cisterns and irrigation systems to create a great fertile demesne round his palace. He chose to be buried at Resafe, but his tomb was destroyed by the victorious Abbasids in 750. Only one member of Hisham's family escaped, his grandson, Abd al-Rahman I, who eventually would seek to recreate near Cordova in Spain the paradise he had known in childhood at Resafe.

22. QALAAT JABER

The substantial Arab castle of Qalaat Jaber was built on a oval hilltop on the left bank of the Euphrates, controlling a key crossing point opposite the Plain of Seffin, scene in 657 of the stand-off between Ali, Muhammad's son-in-law, and Moawiya which led to the marginalization and eventual death of the former and the enduring schism between Sunni and Shi'ite. The position was taken in 1087 by the Seljuk Sultan Malik Shah and subsequently fell to the Crusader county of Edessa (Urfa). Zengi of Aleppo, who took Edessa in 1144, died in a brawl when besieging Jaber two years later. The fortress fell in 1149 and in 1168 Zengi's son, Nur al-Din, began a major programme of reconstruction. Severely damaged by

Qalaat Jaber: brick decoration.

the Mongols, Jaber was restored in 1335–6 for the Mameluke governor of Damascus.

The castle is easily reached from the north end of the Lake Assad Dam. Driving in thick fog, I passed the unmarked turn but was redirected by two puzzled mukhabarat (secret policemen) who were following me. Descending through a re-afforested valley, it is immediately obvious that Lake Assad has enhanced the picturesque claims of the castle, albeit at the expense of compromising its context. The approach is across a narrow isthmus. The partly undercut outcrop, roughly oval, falls away steeply to the south-west, and was defended on the landward side by a ditch. The structure was largely of brick. Much that can be seen dates from after 1972, but elements of the decoration of the towers are original. The entrance and the corridor ramp that climbs to the upper level are largely intact, but little remains within the walls, a solitary minaret apart.

23. MESKENE

The modern town of Meskene has nothing visual to commend it. But to the north-west is a beautiful Ayyubid minaret of the thirteenth century, which certainly merits a detour. A kilometre and a half/almost a mile east of the police post at the eastern end of the town on the Raqqa-to-Aleppo highway, an unmarked road strikes north, beside an irrigation canal; after 4 kilometres/2½ miles a turn to the left leads to the village of Hottin, from the northern side of which the minaret is visible a couple of kilometres/a mile or so away. A good track approaches it from the left.

The minaret stands alone on a ridge from which there must have been spectacular views northwards over the Euphrates valley, now submerged by Lake Assad. The brick minaret, decorated externally with inscriptions, is octagonal: at the centre there is a square core around which climb the stairs – 103 steps survive. The stairs are lit by small windows in alternate sides of the octagon. From the top there is a remarkable prospect over the partly excavated Umayyad mansion which originally occupied the site; the square compound had corner turrets and gateways on the east and west sides which were flanked by rounded turrets. The minaret was most intelligently placed in the centre of the complex when it was moved from its original site before this was flooded by Lake Assad.

Two kilometres/a mile or so to the north, on a promontory now washed by the lake, are the not inconsiderable ruins of a Byzantine settlement. These can, at most times of year, be reached by a track that descends past the minaret. Here, as at Qalaat Jaber, the lake has transformed the context of the site. The descent is through an eroded landscape, almost white in places. By the shore, reed beds have grown up. And two fishermen are in a small boat. The brick structures that promise so well from afar prove to be the remains of the substantial barbican at the north-

west angle of the town walls and their south-western tower. The walls are in the fired brick used so successfully by the Byzantines, protected from rising damp by footings of stone. The walls run eastwards from the fragment of the southern tower, the brick section set above several courses of dressed ashlar. At the extremity of the site is a level space with areas of well-preserved stone paving upon which, rather incongruously, a boat has been drawn up. Of the area originally enclosed by the walls little more than a tenth remains above the waterline, the buildings that have been lost including the so-called qasr and the mosque from which the minaret was salvaged.

What survives is, of course, only the small upper section of a significant Seleucid and Roman town, known by the Byzantines as Barbalissos. The fortifications were part of the Emperor Justinian's ambitious but extravagant scheme to defend Syria from the traditional enemy, the Persians; and they would prove of no avail when the Arabs swept through a century later. As Balis, the place was in about 1100, very briefly, part of the Crusader county of Edessa. The transplanted minaret attests to the continuing importance of the town in the thirteenth century. But subsequently it was largely abandoned in the wake of the Mongol onslaught. Now only the truncated towers of Justinian's fortress and the spectacularly resited minaret preserve the memory of Barbalissos.

The minaret.

24. QALAAT NAJIM

The approach to Qalaat Najim is unforgettable. Seventeen kilometres/10 miles east of the Membij roundabout on the main highway from Aleppo to the Jezira, a road on the right leads in 13 kilometres/8 miles to the castle. As the land falls away towards Lake Assad, the skeleton of a mosque and a maqam rise above a graveyard. Almost immediately the castle comes into sight, with its glacis and battered walls on a rounded hill, caught in a shaft of sunlight against a leaden sky. The lake now rises almost to the level of the walls, but originally the fortress stood proud, high above the Euphrates.

The castle protected an ancient entrepôt on the river, the Roman Caeciliana, now engulfed by the lake. An earlier stronghold was apparently reinforced by Nur al-Din. But, as inscriptions by the entrance establish, the castle as we see it was substantially rebuilt for al-Zaher Ghazi, who as governor of Aleppo also restored the citadel there. The two are the most formidable surviving Arab castles of the Crusader period in Syria. As at Aleppo, the wall and glacis are wrapped around a steeply sloping hill. At Najim it was only necessary for this to be protected by a moat on the landward side.

The entrance is from the south, where the ground falls steeply away. The stair and bridge are modern. The gate is on the right of the three-sided re-entrant. It opens to a vaulted gallery of two bays, from which a second gallery on the left is reached. Optimum use was made of the substantial but not unlimited space above, and on successive levels. A circuit to the left leads from a hammam of three rooms with a steam bath – conveniently beside the kitchen – to a beautiful small residence

The mosque.

arranged around a courtyard with a fountain and three iwans. Equally impressive is a corridor in the form of a ramp with storerooms at either side, some with attachments for tethering animals. Higher up there are a number of large galleries. And from the top of the walls there are spectacular prospects over the lake and northwards towards the modern tomb of the greatest of Ottoman sultans, Suleiman I.

According to the helpful custodian there are Byzantine tombs on the hillside behind the castle. But for those with time to spare a higher priority should be the buildings by the graveyard. The roofless, skeletal mosque is rather more interesting than its modest scale might lead one to expect, for on the walls there are numerous graffiti of daggers and swords, some schematic but others more elaborate. The best-preserved specimens are on the sides of the recess in the south wall. The age of such scratchings is not easily determined, but that of some at least seems to be considerable; others, of course, including those of vehicles, are relatively fresh. The building near by is almost equally rewarding. It is a mausoleum, the tomb chamber opening off a small domed structure with fine honeycombed pendentives. The external walls, notably that to the south, are also covered in graffiti, including more of weaponry. These were apparently not made until long after Qalaat Najim had ceased to be garrisoned, for by the fourteenth century, in the aftermath of the Mongol occupation, Najim was sinking towards the obscurity from which it has now been so tactfully reclaimed by the Syrian Department of Antiquities.

Graffiti of swords.

25. ALEPPO

Aleppo is, with Sana'a in the Yemen and, perhaps, Fez in Morocco, one of the cities in which we can feel closest to the medieval Islamic world. Its souks retain a mystery and a magic that seem all the more potent when one recognizes that almost all of their merchandise is of strictly local interest. This was not the case during the long centuries after Aleppo succeeded Antioch as the main entrepôt between central Asia and the Mediterranean coast, when Shakespeare could despatch a sailor to the city and colonies of merchants from Venice, France and England were established there. The threads of Aleppo's history are numerous, and the patient sightseer will enjoy untangling some of them. But, however essential it is to have a reasonable plan of the city, there is a good deal to be said for getting somewhat lost in it. Try to allow at least two days for your exploration of the town. If you have longer at your disposal, Abdallah Hadjar's *Historical Monuments of Aleppo*, available at the museum and elsewhere, has itineraries and maps which in some areas supplement those in Burns's *Monuments of Syria.*

Aleppo is first recorded, as Halap, nearly four thousand years ago, when it was the capital of the Amorite kingdom of Yamkhad. The temple of the god Hadad on the hill on which the citadel was subsequently built was clearly a key element of the early city and was reconstructed under the neo-Hittites. Halap was subsequently controlled by the Assyrians and the Persians. The latter were defeated by Alexander the Great, after whose death the city became part of the kingdom of Seleucus I Nicator. Halap, renamed Beroia, was greatly enlarged from its original tell, and laid out under the Seleucids on a Hippodamian grid plan, much of which survives, as does the western line of the city wall.

Syria fell to the Romans in 64 BC and Beroia enjoyed a long prosperity as the centre of a productive agricultural area. This was sustained under Byzantine rule. Taken by the Arabs in AD 637, Aleppo came to be overshadowed by Damascus and Baghdad. Sacked by the Byzantines in 962 and hemmed in by Crusader forces from 1098, Aleppo owed its revival from 1128 onwards to the rule of Zengi, the Atabeq of Mosul (1128–46), and his son, Nur al-Din. On the death of the latter's son in 1183 control passed to Saladin, whose energetic son, al-Zaher Ghazi, Malik of Aleppo from 1193 until 1215, rebuilt the citadel. Ayyubid rule ended with the Mongol invasion of 1260. Syria then fell to the Mamelukes, who were to prove assiduous, both as builders and at concentrating trade in their city. The Ottomans, who held Syria from 1516, were equally determined to maintain Aleppo's position. The city's population has grown dramatically since the late nineteenth century and the historic centre is now surrounded by an expanding urban sprawl. It is greatly to the credit of the civil authorities and those who have championed the cause that in recent decades much has been done to preserve and revitalize a unique survival.

For no better reason than that I have usually stayed in the atmospheric and congenial Baron Hotel to the north-west of the walled city, my natural instinct is to approach Aleppo from that direction, entering the walled city from the Bab Antaki, the Antioch Gate, built under the last of the Ayyubids, Yusuf II, governor from 1242 to 1260, and flanked by two impressive hexagonal bastions. Ahead is the modest al-Tuteh Mosque, built into the fragment of the Roman triumphal arch that served as it were as a frontispiece to the decumanus. Before continuing along this, turn to the left and climb the tell of the early settlement. By the city wall is the small Mosque of Qaiqan, with much ancient material set into the external masonry.

The great covered souk of Aleppo, the Suq al-Atarin, follows the decumanus. The narrow openings to the shops lining this preserve the dimensions of those that developed between the columns flanking the street. On a first visit it is best to stick to the main souk, savouring the experience of the crowd and the cries of the street vendors while trying to avoid the attentions of carpet sellers, however desperate they seem. The first section is covered with a metal roof. Beyond this is the first vaulted section in front of the Al-Bahramiye Mosque of 1580. It is worth making a brief detour down the lane beside the eastern wall of this to see the portal, just beyond the mosque on the right, of the Bimaristan, or hospital, founded by Nur al-Din in about 1150–4: the unrestored Kufic dedication is perhaps the most beautiful of the many inscriptions of the kind in Aleppo. As Suq al-Atarin gradually climbs, it becomes more crowded and the shops more colourful. In the eastern section you pass the Madrasa Shazbaktiye, the portal on the right partly covered by the vault of the souk. Go through this, and down the steps of a small vaulted vestibule to the calm of the courtyard. In the prayer room there is a fine early thirteenth-century mirhab of the golden local marble, set off with black and a grey-streaked white: the type was hugely popular in Aleppo and this example is signed by the brothers Abi al-Raja and Abi Abdullah. The souk finally emerges in front of the citadel, which crowns an oval hill and is unquestionably the greatest monument of Aleppo.

The fortifications are largely due to al-Zaher Ghazi, much of whose work was destroyed by the Mongols in 1260 and again by Timur in 1400. By the time the Mamelukes rebuilt the citadel, it was well within the city walls. The citadel walls seem relatively modest in scale, as one looks up at them above the formidable stone glacis, the massive weight of which was partly anchored by the use of recycled columns. The spectacular entrance is at the south-west. A tower, rebuilt in the sixteenth century, stands forward from the bridge that crosses the moat to the massive entrance tower. This dates from the Mameluke restoration programme of 1290–3, although the more richly decorated upper tier was added in

The entrance to the citadel.

the sixteenth century. The gateway, on the right of the opening between the projecting towers, leads to the first of five grand halls that ascend within the gatehouse, each placed for defensive reasons at a right angle to the last, the gates to two of them decorated with lions. The upper level of the tower, approached through an elegant courtyard or by stairs from the first section of the gate, contains the vast, largely restored throne room.

A path crosses the citadel: on the right is the stair down to a series of three cisterns and beyond this the impressive remains of the palace of al-Zaher Ghazi's son, al-Aziz, built in 1230, with a spectacular striped façade. Further north is the deep excavation of the Temple of Hadad, the recently discovered reliefs of which will eventually be shown *in situ*. To the left of the path is the Mosque of Abraham, built for Nur al-Din, and beyond, just within the northern wall, the unexpectedly modest but spare and muscular Great Mosque, rebuilt in 1214 by al-Zaher Ghazi. To the east of this, built against the fortress wall, is the barracks. This dates from 1834, when Syria was held by Muhammed Ali, and now houses a well-arranged museum. From the circuit of the walls there are views across the city, and over the two detached bastions, hanging as it were on the glacis, which were added in the fourteenth century.

Among the buildings to the south of the citadel are Sinan's impressive Khosrofiye Mosque of 1537–46, the sturdy minaret of which has a band of tiled decoration similar to that above the windows of the prayer hall, and the fourteenth-century Hammam al-Nasri, the most spectacular bath complex in Syria. This was until recently in regular use, and on a winter's evening would be crowded with family parties of up to three generations, and with groups of youths joshing, quite unaware of the distinction of the building to which they gave continual life.

The visitor who spares only a day for Aleppo may want to return to the souk and explore the area around the Great Mosque, but there is much to be said for devoting a full day to orientating oneself and seeing at least the key buildings of the walled city and its immediate environs. On a street behind the hammam is the elegant Mameluke al-Otrush Mosque of 1403: this is usually only open at the hours of prayer. The rich façade exploits decorative motifs including a variant of the dogtooth so familiar from northern Romanesque architecture; and the minaret, with two galleries rather than the original three, is equally fine. A few blocks to the east, on the line of the original city wall, is the Altun Bogha Mosque of 1318, the restrained entrance to which leads down to a courtyard of admirable severity. A street to the south-west of the al-Otrush Mosque runs to the Bab al-Maqam. Beyond this continue in the same general direction, passing a number of distinguished domed mausolea, to what Burns fairly calls the 'most beautiful' of Aleppan mosques, the Madrasa Faradis, built in 1234–7 for the widow of al-Zaher Ghazi. The exterior is restrained, but the entrance corridor turns into a particularly elegant colonnaded courtyard: ahead is the triple-domed prayer hall and opposite this a great iwan.

With a map it is not difficult to pick your way back to the walls. Aim for Bab Qinnasrin – the gate leading to the Roman Chalcis, to the west of which is a tract of the wall with two well-restored monumental towers. The open ground outside the gate is due to be transformed into a garden by the Aga Khan Foundation. Although its western bastion has been demolished, the gate, in three sections, remains the grandest of those of the city. Within this, take the road ahead. On the right is the Maristan Arghun al-Kamili of 1354, surely one of the most sophisticated asylums of its date, with a main courtyard and smaller enclosed courts for the inmates. Further on a passage to the right leads to one of the many surprises of Aleppo, the al-Adeliye Mosque, built for an Ottoman governor, Muhammed Pasha, in 1555. This was designed by Sinan with an exacting precision that can only have been exercised by remote control. The double arcade leading to the domed prayer hall is wholly Turkish in conception. Here, and in the mosque itself, there are panels of tiles

The Madrasa Faradis.

with texts from the Koran framed by floral motifs in blue, turquoise and touches of red. The mirhab of coloured marbles is also unusually fine. If the guardian is about, he may offer to take you up to the roof, from which there are marvellous views over the souks.

On the left, just before the road reaches the decumanus, is the handsome domed entrance to the sixteenth-century Khan al-Nahasin where, against all probability, the Venetian consulate survives, little changed since the fall of the Serenissima in 1797, in the south-east corner. There are numerous other khans in Aleppo, many still in use as warehouses or workshops, their doors sheathed with overlapping metal plates and studs. Much the largest, the Khan al-Gumruk, is a block to west. Finished in 1574, this originally housed the French, Dutch and English merchants who made Aleppo their base and is said to have contained no fewer than 344 shops. The entrance is particularly elaborate. The narrow street between the two khans continues obliquely to the north, emerging by the west wall of the Great Mosque. Opposite the side entrance to this is the Madrasa Halawiye. A block incorporating a Byzantine cross must have been deliberately placed beside the steps leading down to it. Across the courtyard is the domed prayer hall, with a curving row of columns with spectacularly carved capitals: this is all that survives of the sixth-century Cathedral of St Helena.

The Great Mosque was founded by the Umayyad Caliph al-Walid I in about 715, but was largely rebuilt under the indefatigable Nur al-Din after a fire in 1160. Subsequently the Mamelukes modified the arcades of the courtyard. The minaret, which happily survived the fire, was built in 1090–2 under the Seljuk Sultan Tutush. The tower is treated in four tiers, divided by horizontal bands of Kufic script; the decoration of the sections differs but is coordinated with great skill. On my first visit at the time of the First Gulf War, I was rather taken aback to be told in the courtyard by an irate youth that he wished to kill me for what the Allies were then doing to the people of Baghdad – the only hint of aggression I have ever experienced in Syria. Normally the mood is very different: on a sunny winter's afternoon, women occupy the northern arcade, while men make do with that on the east, three of the arches of which are again of dogtooth pattern. The great treasure of the prayer hall is the splendid fifteenth-century wooden mimbar enriched with ivory to the right of the mirhab. To the left of this in a shrine sheathed with blue tiles is the head of Zaccharius, the father of St John the Baptist, whose relics are revered at Damascus, for Muslim cities could be as competitive in such matters as their Christian counterparts. Magnificent as the Great Mosque is, the hand of the restorer is too heavily felt.

The Madrasa Othmaniye.

The east entrance of the mosque leads to the Suq al-Manadil. Some way down on the left is a rare survival of Ayyubid Aleppo, the public latrine. Restored in 1357, this now needs attention. Just beyond, at the end of the first block, is the Mameluke Khan al-Sabun, with a lavishly decorated entrance. From the upper arcade of the courtyard the citadel can be seen, floating above the city. Sometimes it is possible to get access to the roof, a forgotten world of satellite dishes and air-conditioning units, festooned with wires, where a man may be feeding his pigeons or releasing them to circle above the city. On leaving the khan, turn north to reach a small square. On the east side of this is another notable caravanserai, the seventeenth-century Khan al-Wazir, with a fine frontispiece and a large courtyard on two levels; the section on the north is a recent replacement.

For, while much of the pattern of medieval Aleppo survives, the area to the north of the Great Mosque has been ruthlessly cut through to make way for a road. This was part of an ill-conceived programme that has sensibly been abandoned. Beyond this scar there are more buildings of interest. Cross the new road and take that opposite the east end of the Khan al-Wazir. Following this you reach the Khan Qurt Bey, which was begun in 1493 and is perhaps the most atmospheric building of its type in the city. Beyond this cross another of the disruptive new streets and continue to the Bab al-Nasr, or Gate of Triumph, which was restored by al-Zaher Ghazi in 1212. The lane to the east of the gate leads to the Madrasa Othmaniye. Built in 1730–8, this has an unexpectedly spacious courtyard, with forty-two rooms for scholars and large iwans flanking the mosque: a ginger cat watches from a plastic chair and a student emerges from his lair. West of the Bab al-Nasr is the seventeenth-century Beit Junblatt, built by a governor of Aleppo to an appropriate scale. Huge iwans dominate the commensurate court. In the past an unmistakable air of decay did not diminish the charm of the place, but it has recently been restored and is now not readily accessible.

The areas beyond the Bab al-Nasr hold much of interest. The first turning on the right off the street opposite the gate leads to the beautiful late Mameluke archway of the otherwise demolished Utch Khan. Through this can be seen the Masbanat al-Zanabili, a soap factory still in use within another Mameluke khan, which can be reached from the lane to the east. To the north-west is the Harami quarter, in which many early houses survive.

Few tourists trouble with the north-east section of the walled city. But this also is rewarding. At the corner of the enceinte, by a busy intersection, is the Bab al-Hadid, the southern section of which survives, leading to one of the more rewarding streets of Aleppo, the Sharia al-Bayada. This runs through the Mameluke Suq al-Haddadi, now used by metalworkers and carpenters, and passes a number of public buildings, notably the Al-Sarawi Mosque of 1402 with its beautiful façade. But it is the survival of so many private houses with their wooden kishets – extensions on the upper floor that stretch out over the road to catch the wind – that makes the street so appealing. The road climbs and after a final turn you are almost surprised to be confronted by the eastern end of the citadel.

To the north-west of the walled city is the Jdeide Quarter, favoured since late Mameluke times by Aleppo's Christians. This would be a good place from which to launch yourself on a second day's circuit. The best approach is from Tilel Street, north of the eccentric clock tower of 1899 and the lamentable Sheraton Hotel. The churches of the various denominations are concentrated near the prominent building of the Maronites. More distinguished are the houses of the quarter. Among the finest is Beit Ajiqbash of 1757, now the Museum of Popular Traditions. The main room on the north of the courtyard is unusually ambitious, with a prettily decorated ceiling. Forty metres/130 feet north, on Jdeide Street, is Beit Ghazale, now an Armenian school. At the time of my first visit the iwan was festooned with rows of portraits of President Assad, a testimony to the gratitude of Christian Aleppo to one of the few leaders in the Near East who consistently protected the interests of minorities.

No visitor to Aleppo should neglect the National Museum, to the west of the walled city. The entrance is a reconstruction of the gateway of a temple of the ninth century BC from Tell Halaf, with awkward animals supporting clumsy caryatids. The main sequence is inevitably chronological. Sir Max Mallowan's campaigns at Tell Brak yielded material from 3000 BC onwards: stone rosettes, figurines and representations of animals, as well as a section of an elaborate frieze from the Eye Temple. The finds from Mari are visually more remarkable: moulds with birds and animals; an expressive figure of a spring goddess with a vase of water; a crisp statuette of a man in a skirt of leaves; and a crumpled bronze lion that guarded the Temple of Dagon (2000–1800 BC). Equally rich is the material from Ugarit: a gold bowl, shown upside down, with lions and deer and scenes from the chase; bronzes which imply a knowledge of Egypt; and weights of animal forms.

The long gallery at the back of the museum is arranged in three sections. There is more crude sculpture in unyielding basalt from Tell Halaf: least unappealing perhaps is the scorpion-cum-bird man from the Scorpion Gate of the palace. Another Aramaean city, Arslan Tash, yielded elements of a royal bed. It is evident that the craftsmen, while influenced by their Assyrian counterparts, were also aware of developments in the Phoenician coastal cities and in Egypt. In the final section of the room are substantial sculptures from Tell Ahmar, including a large stela of a king with supplicants, and impressive lions that guarded the gates of the palace. This was built in the mid-ninth century BC, when Tell Ahmar was a significant administrative centre of the Assyrian Empire.

In the next gallery there are energetic reliefs from the Aramaic temple at Ain Dara, celebrating the mountain god, Samas. Much work continues to be done on the archaeological sites of northern Syria, and the cases of finds from these merit at least cursory inspection. The later material in the museum is, in general, less remarkable. Among the objects of the Roman period there is an unusual pottery vessel with human heads from Raqqa. The Palmyrene funerary portraits are not of particular distinction; but a Parthian statue of a skirted man is more unusual, yet another reminder of the complicated cross-currents that determined Syria's past.

Aleppo is the obvious base from which to visit the 'dead cities' and other sites of northern Syria covered in the following sections. The visitor with time might also like to make a brief visit to Qinnasrin, some 30 kilometres/19 miles to the south and easily reached from the motorway. The modern town spreads over the site of the Roman Chalcis ad Belum, and youths play football on the large irregular citadel tell to the south, of which traces of the Byzantine walls survive. Surveying the sweeping prospect of the semi-desert beyond on a clear afternoon it is not difficult to understand why the place was so important to Roman and Byzantine Syria.

It was from Chalcis that key routes crossed the desert to Palmyra and Resafe. There were substantial settlements at Khanazir, on the road from Aleppo to Isriya, and on a route further east, touching the margin of the salt lake, or Sabkhat, an area of particular beauty with villages of traditional beehive houses. There are a number of small tells beside this. By the fourth of these, 20 kilometres/12½ miles south-east of Sfire, to the north of Umm al-Amud, is Hatleh, where numerous fragments of the Byzantine door frames and columns are scattered among the mud houses, many of which were built round cores of recycled stones.

Twenty kilometres/12½ miles further on turn left, and continue for some 14 kilometres/9 miles to reach Zabed, now a sprawling village of beehive houses but once a substantial town, where a wide wadi debouches from the hills to the west. Round the *pise* (mud) houses there is a scattering of basalt column drums and elements of doors, and to the left of the southern track into the village four basalt arches, which presumably supported a small dome, poke up behind a house. The Byzantine town stretched up the wadi bed. At the centre there was a rectangular citadel, and near this a very ruined church can be seen. Much of the plan of the town can still be understood, as the white stone foundations of the walls stand out against the darker soil and the thin green grass. Higher up the wadi on the right is an elegant mausoleum, with a dedicatory inscription. But intriguing as such remains are, Zabed is most memorable for the beauty of the country through which it is reached.

26. CYRRHUS

No visitor to Cyrrhus will forget the approach. The road from Aleppo by way of Azaz is easily found, although once I took a wrong turning to find myself surrounded by perplexed conscripts at a border post, and had to wait for higher authority to allow me to retreat. The undulating country is of particular beauty, with olive groves and plantations of Aleppo pines. Some 26 kilometres/16 miles beyond Azaz the road crosses the river Afrin on a handsome Roman bridge with two piers. These have triangular beaks facing upstream and are rounded behind; the paving may have been largely replaced. A kilometre/half a mile further on a second somewhat less well-preserved Roman, or Byzantine, bridge, of six arches, spans the Subun Suyu.

Cyrrhus lies on higher ground to the west of the river. The position was chosen by that indefatigable founder of cities Seleucus I Nicator; but with the eclipse of the Seleucids Cyrrhus declined, only to recover under Roman rule in the first century AD. A legion was stationed here until AD 64, and the city continued to be of some military importance until the third century. The city's Byzantine name, Hagiopolis, was not unconnected with the cult of the local martyrs Cosmos and Damian, patron saints of doctors and thus of the Medici. Justinian reinforced the defences against the Sasanian threat, but it was, of course, to the Arabs that Cyrrhus fell in 637. The site continued to be inhabited and as Coricia was held by the short-lived Crusader county of Edessa in the eleventh century, but has long since been abandoned.

The visitor arrives at the partly reconstructed South Gate, which was a structure of considerable elegance, the approach paved with basalt. The walls of Roman Cyrrhus enclosed a roughly triangular area, dominated on the west by a substantial hill. Make for this. The Seleucid acropolis was largely reconstructed for Justinian, whose masons took full advantage of what they found but were of course constrained by the fall of the ground. Much of the Byzantine masonry has fallen, but recent work in the south-eastern section gives an idea of the scale on which the citadel was reconstructed. Descending from this, the city wall can be followed in a north-eastward direction towards the river. A substantial enclosure was built within it. Beyond this the wall turns to run eastwards, following a slope that protected the position from the valley floor. The North Gate, although substantial, was less elaborate than its counterpart. Within this are the remains of a basilica and large church. South of these a row of column drums level with the ground marks the line of the cardo maximus which ran between the two gates.

Set back from the cardo and below the acropolis hill is the handsome theatre, which has been partly reconstructed. Built in the second century, this is the great monument of Roman Cyrrhus. Originally marginally larger than its counterpart at Bosra, the theatre has been severely damaged by earthquakes. The lower tier of the seating, with fourteen rows of benches rising in eleven sections, survives, as it was cut back into the hillside, but the upper level was more vulnerable and has long since been largely robbed: two tumbled benches each with an arm decorated with a fish motif were evidently not thought worth recycling. Although most of the marble base of the frontispiece of the stage building remains in place, most of the structure fell into the orchestra in a picturesque jumble: a column of imported green marble, a Corinthian capital and numerous fragments of the richly carved entablature.

Beyond the South Gate is a particularly impressive tower tomb of two storeys crowned by a six-sided pyramidal roof, the topmost element of which is decorated with acanthus. Apparently of the second or third century, this is now incorporated in the mosque built for pilgrims to the tomb of a Muslim saint who was buried in the lower chamber of the tomb in the fourteenth century. A tenebrous stair mounts to the upper level, the great arched openings of which frame views over a graveyard and fields, in which the luxuriant greens of the crops stand out against the dark brown soil.

View from the mausoleum.

27. AIN DARA

The river Afrin, the ancient Oinoparas, which rises in the Kartal Dagi, north of Cyrrhus across the Turkish border, drains to the Plain of Amuq, north-east of Antioch, which is also fed by the Karasu and the Orontes. Like these the Afrin has brought prosperity to its valley, and south of the sleepy eponymous town there are numerous orchards. The unexpectedly high tell of Ain Dara rises abruptly from the valley floor, some 10 kilometres/6 miles south of the town.

The site was first occupied in the Bronze Age and remained in intermittent use until well into the medieval era. Scattered fragments testify to its layered history. But it is for what we learn about one phase of this that Ain Dara is so memorable. Occupying much of the north-western section of the summit of the mound is the substantial carcass of a major Neo-Hittite temple of the tenth to ninth centuries BC. As a cult statue excavated in 1980 is thought to establish, this was dedicated to Ishtar, the fertility goddess of the Semitic pantheon.

The main approach was from the south. The processional way was guarded by a pair of flanking lions, of a type familiar from many Neo-Hittite sites, but which in this instance may symbolize the goddess. One, disconcertingly well preserved, still stands, but the other is on its side. The plan of the temple itself is understood best from the higher ground to the south, a rectangle, with steps mounting to two successive enclosures, of which the second was the larger. Many of the blocks of black basalt, alas, have suffered badly from flaking, but enough of the structure survives to offer a good idea of the power of the original elevation, the upper sections of which were of mud brick that has inevitably left no trace. Lions appear with sphinxes in the monumental frieze of the lower section of the façade and in the vestibule to the entrance; above these were

Neo-Hittite architectural sculpture.

larger lions seen from the front, of which little more than the claw-like paws survive. Much of the original paving of the temple remains in place. Cut into a large slab at the entrance to the outer enclosure are the outsize prints of two feet; on the next slab there is a single left foot. Their precise significance is uncertain. But parallels can be cited in other Iron Age contexts, including the much later fort at Dunadd in Argyllshire, Scotland; and we can speculate as to how such footprints served to link worshipper and deity. Ignorant as we are of their full meaning, the lapidary footprints at Ain Dara make us feel almost uncomfortably close to a very distant world.

28. QALAAT SEMAAN: ST SIMEON

The great monastery of St Simeon is one of the wonders of Syria. Set on a high promontory to the east of the valley of the Afrin, it lies at the heart of the series of so-called 'dead cities' – the prosperous agricultural communities that flourished under Byzantine rule – and became one of the major cult centres of the Eastern Church. The warm limestone masonry is of a haunting beauty.

It is not easy in our secular age to comprehend how key a role St Simeon had for his contemporaries. Born about 390, he entered a monastery at Telanissos, now Deir Semaan, in his early twenties. A fervent masochist, he in time retreated to a column built to generous specifications, some 20 metres/66 feet high and up to 2 metres/7 feet wide, set on the ridge above the town. Happily unaware of the eloquent ridicule his calling as a stylite would inspire in Gibbon, Simeon remained at his post until he died in 459. His fervour was matched by a gift for what would now be termed self-promotion, and Simeon's column became a place of pilgrimage in his lifetime. Simeon's unyielding conservatism must have been reassuring to the imperial authorities at a time when the Monophysite heresy had taken a strong hold in Syria. After his death his body was taken to Antioch, and eventually to Constantinople. Nonetheless the Emperor Zeno (474–91) was associated with the prodigious project to construct the huge basilica around the column, which largely dates from the 480s and was one of the signal architectural achievements of the age.

The processional route was from Deir Semaan, where most of the pilgrims were catered for, and is marked by a triumphal arch. Today the tourist arrives from the east, entering through the ticket office beside the

St Simeon: the narthex to the basilica.

outer wall of the enclosure, which is of the tenth century. Most will go straight to the church. But if time permits, turn south and keep towards the western wall of the enclosure, following the original approach in reverse to the propylaeum at the end of the southern extension of this, before returning to the baptistery on the right of the route. Within the roughly square structure is a central octagon. At the east end of this is a small apse to which converts were conducted through lateral passages to be baptised. To the south of the baptistery is a small basilica, apparently an early addition.

From the baptistery the pilgrim advanced towards the basilica. Trees now give shade. The terraced ground slopes gently upwards. The church is preceded by a narthex of unexpected elegance and originality, with a wide central arch, opening to paired door-cases to the basilica, flanked by a smaller arch at either side, placed before the doorways to the aisles. Much of the detail is of Roman origin, but the windswept acanthus capitals have broken from the straitjacket of the Corinthian order: the type would be used in other buildings of the period and find a last echo in the fourteenth-century Mosque of al-Tavashi at Aleppo.

Entering the basilica, one is inevitably surprised by its size. At the heart of the cruciform complex is what remains of St Simeon's column, eroded by time and relic hunters. A great octagon was constructed round it, with wide arches supported on piers flanked by columns, again with flying acanthus capitals. The design was clearly intended to ensure the maximum visibility of the column. The arches on the main axes open to the four basilicas: those at the diagonals frame exedras and lead to subsidiary arches to the basilicas. As one moves, the perspective of the arches is rearranged. The heaviness of the piers is explained by their function – to sustain the original roof, which fell in an earthquake of 528 and was not replaced. The basilica to the east, 43 metres/140 feet in length as against

The basilica, with the column of St Simeon.

the 30 metres/100 feet of its counterparts, was set some degrees off the axis of the rest of the building to be correctly orientated: it was clearly used for the main religious services. The western basilica is built out over the great terrace that was constructed to support the structure. The view over the valley of the Afrin and a scattering of Byzantine villages is unforgettable. Sounds rise and a bird of prey searches out its next meal.

Walk on through the northern basilica to climb up to the small mortuary chapel beside the enclosure wall. On your return, the exterior of the eastern basilica deserves attention. As at Qalb Lozeh, the three apses are not set within the structure but project, in anticipation of later Romanesque architecture in the west, and are adorned with small columns, here in two tiers. The outer south wall of the basilica is particularly happy in the balance between the lunette-surmounted doors and the generous cornice that runs round the arched windows. Beside this is a chapel, which was presumably associated with the adjoining monastery, the well-preserved façades of which form a large, irregular courtyard. It is thought that this complex was reserved for priests.

St Simeon is very much on the tourist route. But it is a large site that can absorb large numbers, particularly when these are dragooned by tour guides. This is hardly surprising, for the place would originally have had all the facilities of a popular attraction.

29. DEIR SEMAAN, QATURA, SITT AL-RUM AND REFADE

The concentration of Byzantine buildings in the Jebel Semaan is by any standard extraordinary. The visitor to St Simeon from Aleppo will already have seen the imposing and remarkably preserved fifth-century church of Mushabbak above the road, and on the approach to the basilica other of the 'dead cities' come into view. A kilometre or so/half a mile short of St Simeon, a track on the right leads to the ruins of Takleh, with a beautiful mid-fifth-century church, the west front of which with windows on three levels stands out high on the ridge. Yet more appealing is the cluster of villages below and to the south-west of the basilica.

The logical place to commence is Deir Semaan, the pilgrimage town that grew up below the now rebuilt monumental arch at the foot of the processional way to St Simeon. Some 150 metres/164 yards to the south of the arch is the vast ruin of the Pandocheion, the larger of two such complexes, where pilgrims stayed. This is similar to the monastery associated with the basilica. In spring the small cultivated plots that surround it are carpeted with pink weeds. There are numerous early buildings round the houses of the modern village, but two monasteries to the west of this are of greater appeal.

The South-West Monastery, assigned by Professor Butler to the sixth century, is memorable for the beautiful and unusually complete church. The west front stands to full height, and the lateral façades are particularly effective, the arched windows of the clerestory linked by a continuous cornice of the type so characteristic of the area. The annexed buildings, with simple colonnaded fronts, were no doubt intended for the use of pilgrims. Much of the masonry must have been cut from two small quarries not far away. In spring the little fields near by are almost luridly green and there is a scattering of fiercely blue irises. The North-West Monastery, an even larger complex, is further from the village. Behind the rather battered church there is a rock-cut necropolis in the form of a colonnaded courtyard entered through a narthex.

A track from Deir Semaan is marked to Refade, but it is perhaps more rewarding – and less axle-challenging – to return to the main road and follow this southwards for 2 kilometres/just over 1 mile, turning right for Qatura. On the approach there is an impressive tower. Beyond the village the road, which leads to the 'dead city' of Zarzita, passes a low cliff into which a series of tombs were carved. The sculptures are of modest quality but reflect the dissemination of Roman taste in the area. On the hillside to the south of the city is an altogether more sophisticated monument, with two columns surmounted by a cornice. This bears an inscription of AD 195 to one Aemilius Reginus, who was evidently buried in the associated tomb chamber.

It is difficult not to suppose that the form of the monument was inspired by that of AD 152 to a young auxiliary on the staff of the governor of Syria called Isidotos Ptolemaus at Sitt al-Rum, hardly a kilometre/two-thirds of a mile to the north and most easily reached by a track from the centre of Qatura. Here the columns are square, and originally decorated with inset panels. There were fifteen sarcophagi in the associated subterranean tomb chamber. A little to the north, near the road, is one of the earlier churches in the area, probably of the fourth century, elegant in its simplicity and unexpectedly narrow in relation to its height. Isolated as this now is, the place has a particular charm, not least when the ubiquitous blue irises seem to compete with red anemones.

The road continues to Refade, which is already in sight. To Butler this was 'the most picturesque of all the little deserted cities of the hill country' and for Burns it 'almost' evoked 'a deserted Tuscan hill village'.

Deir Semaan, South-West Monastery: the church.

At the highest point is a massive tower, some 9 metres/30 feet high. From here a path curls to the village, which consists of a number of surprisingly commodious houses with dependencies and outbuildings. The going is quite rough, and it comes as a surprise to find that the nearest of the houses, with an elegant colonnaded façade now filled in with recent walls, is in use. The buildings are mostly of the sixth century, and their sophistication may reflect the relative agricultural richness of the area, even before the heyday of the olive industry. There is no sign of a church, which suggests that the one at Sitt al-Rum remained in service. But the early inhabitants of Refade must always have been aware of the proximity of the great monastery of St Simeon that crowns the ridge to the east.

Qatura: the tomb of Aemilius Reginus.

30. KHARRAB SHAMS, KALLOTTO AND BARAD

Sightseeing among the 'dead cities' is a happy addiction. The massif to the north-east of Qalaat Semaan is gratifyingly rich in remains. From the monastery turn left and continue eastwards, through the villages of Basofan, with a number of Byzantine ruins hemmed in among the modern buildings, and Burj Haidar, with the skeleton of an arcaded church beside the road and other buildings, including a tower and, at the eastern fringe of the modern settlement, an elaborate chapel. After some 20 kilometres/12½ miles the eminently picturesque ruins of Kharrab Shams come into view to the north. A turn on the left leads to the site.

Kharrab Shams cascades down the southern slope of a low hill. The most conspicuous monument is the beautiful fourth-century church, which may have been partly reconstructed a century later, at the foot of the hill. Set behind a now ruinous narthex, the west front has windows of differing scale at four levels, almost but not precisely symmetrical in arrangement. The aisles have fallen, but the arcaded nave survives with its complement of clerestory windows, six on the earlier north side and no fewer than ten opposite. The nearby trees enhance the charm of the place. Behind the church are the remains of numerous houses of rather rough polygonal blocks, many built into the hillside and all indifferently preserved. The usual ingenious channels to catch water can be traced. And even the most assiduous Byzantinist will be beguiled by the wildflowers, from grape hyacinths to poppies. At the top of the slope is a well-preserved chapel of the sixth century, the back wall of which is cut from the bedrock. Such details as the crosses of the south door and the capitals are competently carved.

Kharrab Shams is at its most magical in the evening, when the carcass

Kharrab Shams.

of the church is at its most dramatic. One April, as I sat musing behind the chapel while the light drained from a cloudy sky, hundreds of geese flew noisily overhead. As they passed I was aware of rifle shots and then of the shouts of a dozen youths, running in pursuit. Their quarry escaped and I became their trophy, escorted in triumph to the spot where an older man was preparing their food on a fire. Instruments were played and the boys began to dance in the firelight. Then one of them asked me to read the logo on his leather jacket and the others joined in the game. From mere garments we graduated to their guns, one from Italy, another from Turkey: their cartridges proved to be from Czechoslovakia. Hungry as I was, I accepted the smallest possible morsel of their delicious chicken and took off as the youths resumed their dance, hoping that they would be pleased with the bag of oranges I left in their pick-up.

From Kharrab Shams one can see the enticing ruin of Qalaat Kallotto on a ridge 2 kilometres or so/1 mile to the north-west. Recent quarrying has scarred the valley, but the walk is satisfying, not least when one comes across the ancient and partly rock-cut tracks. And the very substantial church, built on the site of a Roman temple, is most impressive. The west front is severe. The interior is choked with fallen blocks, but the masonry is of consistently fine quality. The nave was divided from the aisles by fluted Corinthian columns, and screened from the apse. With field glasses one can survey the ruins of Barad, and the nearer complex of Kaffoinabo, some 2 kilometres/1 mile to the west.

Barad was the largest Byzantine settlement in the area, and a major centre for the production of olive oil and other agricultural crops. While the walk from Kharrab Shams would be rewarding, Barad is more conveniently reached from a turn to the right 14 kilometres/9 miles from Deir Semaan on the road to Afrin or from a newer road marked from the highway north of Aleppo. Barad was a Roman town, the wealth of which is suggested by the beautiful funerary monument, perhaps of the third century, to the north of the modern village. Near by is a roughly contemporary bath building in a surprisingly complete state. Further on are the elegant church of 561 and the tantalizing ruins of the cathedral, or Church of Julianus, which was among buildings of the area second in size only to the basilica of St Simeon. The modern Maronite church beside it is unworthy of its context.

Barad: the mausoleum.

At the south-western corner of the town is a further church, small and relatively intact, the arched windows of which are linked by one of the undulating cornices that are so characteristic of local Byzantine building. Half a kilometre/one-third of a mile in the same direction, on a low hill and thus visible from afar, is a sixth-century monastery, with an austere chapel and associated structures including a tower and a residential block. No single building at Barad has the magic of the churches of Kharrab Shams or Kallotto, but the survival of so much of the town is remarkable, not least because the fertility of its hinterland must have always been prized. Barad remains an agricultural community – on my first visit a man was ploughing with donkeys beside the mausoleum – and the rock-cut storerooms of the monastery are still in use.

31. BAQIRHA, BAMUQQA AND QALB LOZEH

The westernmost concentration of 'dead cities' is in the Jebel Barisha and the Jebel al-Ala. A reasonably comprehensive survey of the more rewarding sites might take two days; and while Baqirha, Bamuqqa and Qalb Lozeh are in their differing ways the most significant of these, others can profitably be inserted in the itinerary and so I will briefly touch upon them. The area is reached most conveniently by taking the main road from Aleppo to the Turkish frontier at Bab al-Hawa, which has the merit of passing after some 40 kilometres/25 miles a remarkable section of the Roman road from Antioch to Chalcis: climbing a steep hill in easy stages, this was tactfully restored by the French.

At the roundabout before Bab al-Hawa, a turn to the left is marked to Harim. The first village, Sarmada, has little to commend it despite its Roman tomb, but just after the central crossroads a road on the right is signed to Kseijeya, high on a ridge overlooking the Antioch road, which with its colonnaded rows of shops was clearly a prosperous market town. At the crossroads 4 kilometres/2½ miles beyond Sarmada, a lane on the right turns to the remarkably preserved monastery of Braij, partly cut into the hillside and backed by two deep cisterns: the austerity of the complex is relieved by a colonnade of three tiers. The road on the left leads after 6 kilometres/4 miles to Meez, which was a Roman foundation. The forum is to the right of the road and there are two substantial churches, of which the better preserved is to the east.

Continue on the Harim road and after some 5.5 kilometres/3½ miles Baqirha is marked on the right. The road descends and there are unexpected views over the level Plain of Amuq, across the Turkish border at the foot of the escarpment. Above the village on an outcrop to the

Baqirha: the Temple of Zeus Bombos, from the south-west.

right of the road is the impressive cella of the Temple of Zeus Bombos (of the altar), dated to AD 161 by an inscription. The temple was approached from the east. Only one of the four columns of the portico survives, notable for the elegance of the Corinthian capital. The order was also used for the pilasters of the cella, four on the lateral walls and three at the back, facing the road. A platform to the east and other very fragmentary elements of the compound can be traced.

To judge from the number of olive presses, the hillside must from the second century or so have been heavily planted with olive groves. The ruins of the settlement are substantial. And among the many houses, there are two interesting churches. The earlier, of 501, is ruinous, but the eastern wall, the bema of the nave and an elaborate baptistery remain. Very much more impressive is the Eastern Church, with an inscription of 546. The narthex and west front are in surprisingly good order. The builder did not believe in restraint; and his riot of external mouldings and decorated courses evoked 'drooping spaghetti' for Burns. The internal detail was equally idiosyncratic.

Bamuqqa is reached from the village of Bashmishli, roughly a kilometre/ two-thirds of a mile beyond the Baqirha turn on the Harim road. Turn right on a road that twists among the modern houses and then heads to a sizeable grove of ilexes. Shaded by this is an unusually elegant Roman villa with an external stair leading to the upper floor. This must owe its survival to being selected in 1196, after Nur al-Din had expelled the Crusaders, as the burial site of Sheikh Khalil Sadeq, who is still revered by the Alouites of the village. A fine cistern and a tomb are associated with the villa, which has been variously dated between the first and the third centuries. To the north are no fewer than sixteen more modest houses, of no later than the fifth century. A youth studies the Koran in the shade, while two herdsmen take their animals along the ancient track that leads to the north-west, watering their animals in an early cistern on their way.

Qalb Lozeh can be reached from Harim by a dramatic road that passes the village of Bnabel, where a beautiful Roman house stands to full height, although its Corinthian colonnade has fallen, but the shortest route is to turn south at the main junction in Bashmishli. Just before Barisha there is a sign to the right for Dayhis, a substantial site with numerous houses and at the north-east corner a large but largely fallen church, flanked by a well-preserved baptistery, where the font survives, albeit on its side. Turn right in Barisha for Hattan, and then left before taking the road that climbs the escarpment to the right. At the top of this, hanging over the flank of the jebel, is the almost disconcertingly complete Byzantine village of Kirkbizeh, with a concentration of substantial houses and a small fourth-century church.

Qalb Lozeh is some 2 kilometres/1 mile or so to the south. The substantial Druze village has consumed all the domestic buildings of its predecessor. But happily the prodigious church was spared. Built perhaps soon after the mid-fifth century, this was one of the major achievements of Christian architecture in Syria.

One's first view is from the north, but it makes sense to begin with the west front, flanked by two towers, which were originally linked by the outer arch of a vestibule, the inner wall of which survives. The west door, which is strengthened by an open relieving arch above, leads to the nave. This is separated from the narrower aisles at each side by three wide arches (linked by an undulating cornice) that rest on square piers with capitals of acanthus. The aisles had flat roofs of stone slabs – much of that of the south aisle is in place – which did not take light from the clerestory windows, eleven at either side, alternating with brackets for the now lost columns, the capitals of which underpinned the original roof of wood. The arch framing the raised apse is particularly fine, with chastely decorated pilasters; and the masonry of the semi-dome is equally satisfying. At either side of this are two small rooms, of which that on the right was reserved for priests.

Externally, the church is also impressive. The south front is substantially intact. There are three doors, the larger in the centre, again with relieving arches above. These were protected by roofs, as the evidence of post holes and cuttings indicates. In earlier Syrian churches, apses had been built within the traditional rectangular structures, which took their outward form from Roman temples. At Qalb Lozeh the designer took the bold step of projecting the apse outside the body of the central block, in anticipation of what was to become the norm of Romanesque and Gothic churches in the West. The apse is admirably disciplined in detail, with six generous columns, the three arched windows and a heavy cornice, only part of which is in place. Qalb Lozeh does not disappoint.

Two appealing 'dead cities' are off the road beyond Qalb Lozeh. After some 3 kilometres/2 miles and well before the village of Kafer Killa, a track climbs to the left for Behyo. In the centre of the site is a mid-fifth-century church, of which the end walls are reasonably intact. North-east of this was a later church, originally with side arches like those at Qalb Lozeh, that is less well preserved. Blue irises grow in the paved court to the south. There are numerous olive presses, some of considerable elaboration, many with large bulbous rollers and all with carefully worked-out draining systems.

A kilometre/two-thirds of a mile beyond Kafer Killa, a road to the right is signed to Beshindlaye. This is a place of immense charm, where the presence of the modern village enhances an appreciation of the site, even though many of the Byzantine buildings have suffered as a result. As at Behyo there are numerous olive presses. The most spectacular of these is in a large complex at the south-western corner of the village, entered through a substantial building with arches, between which there is a door. To reach this you pass the tomb built in AD 134 for one Tiberius Claudius Sosandros, whose very name implies perhaps something of his ambition. Marked by a tall monolith, the tomb itself is cut into the rock, and is reached by a wide flight of steps. The façade is decorated with festoons divided by animal heads, which have been largely erased. It now houses stock, and a spade lies by the entrance.

The only church in the jebel that almost competes with Qalb Lozeh is at Dersyta. To get there, go back to the junction outside Hattan and turn right for Korkanaya, from where a road heads south. Dersyta is 5 kilometres/3 miles away, just before the rocky plateau begins to fall away to lower ground. There are a number of houses, but these yield in interest to the church at the eastern angle of the village. Parts of the lateral walls survive to the level of the cornice, but it is in the external treatment of the apse that the church is exceptional. The builder adhered to the convention of flanking the apse with lateral chambers, but did not disguise the curved form of the former externally. The apse, the windows of which as at Qalb Lozeh were divided by pillars, is thus set between the flanking blocks, but does not project beyond these. So the elevation has an almost baroque character, a sense of movement that the continuous cornice does not wholly control. The less successful variant of the pattern at Basofan was begun in 491 and this church may be of similar date. At Dersyta, as at Qalb Lozeh, one senses how interested Syrian builders and their employers were in employing new architectural formulas that had been developed in Antioch and elsewhere.

Qalb Lozeh: the apse.

32. HARIM: HARENCH

Harim is 20 kilometres/12½ miles west of Bab el-Hawa, the main border post between Aleppo and the Hatay. The bustling modern town has grown up on a ridge descending from the Jebel al-Ala, and overlooks the lush and level Plain of Amuq, now in Turkey. To the west is a steep isolated hill, roughly oval in shape. The military potential of this, of controlling access to the Iron Bridge across the Orontes on the main road from Aleppo to Antioch, seems first to have been recognized by the Byzantines under Nicephorus Phocas, who fortified it in 959. The place became a key to the defence of Antioch. Suleiman Ben Qutulmish seized it in 1084, before taking Antioch itself, but within a year the Seljuks intervened.

The Franks in their turn recognized the importance of Harim, which they renamed Harench, when they invested Antioch in 1097 during the First Crusade. They took the castle in November, only to lose it the following February, but recovered it before Antioch finally fell to Bohemund in June 1098. The failure of the Crusaders to take Aleppo meant that Harench, which they reconstructed, became a key outpost of the principality of Antioch. Nur al-Din seized it in 1149. A Crusader army commanded by King Baldwin III of Jerusalem recovered it nine years later, but Nur al-Din reconquered it in 1164, after his victory in the Plain of Artah. Thenceforward Harim posed a direct threat to the Crusaders' control of the Plain of Amuq, and one that became the more menacing after it was reconstructed in 1199 for Saladin's son, the Malik al-Zaher Ghazi, greatest of Arab castle-builders of the time. Antioch fell in 1268. Harim was subsequently sacked by the Mongols and, although it was restored after their withdrawal, was gradually abandoned.

The visitor to Harim must restrain his or her expectations. The castle

Exposed section of the lower level of the south-east tower.

can never have been comparable in distinction with al-Zaher Ghazi's work on the citadel of Aleppo or at Qalaat Najim. The contour of the hill had no doubt been altered by his predecessors, but its sides were evidently cut away to create a glacis of the kind we associate with Ghazi's fortifications, except at the east end, which was protected by a natural cliff. Only a small section of the masonry of the glacis survives, not far from the main entrance at the west end. Below this, and on the east side of the hill, there are sections of the bedrock cut at the appropriate angle.

The main entrance was strongly defended and bears an inscription recording Ghazi's reconstruction. Within the gate there is a long vaulted corridor, flanked by storerooms, similar to its more ambitious counterpart at Qalaat Najim. The last door but one on the left leads to a small and unexpectedly elegant bath complex, with a hypocaust on small stone blocks in the hot room. The corridor mounts to an open area, from which those who do not suffer from claustrophobia can descend the flight of steps on the left that gives access to a very deep well, cut into the bedrock. The keep at the east end and the adjacent towers are very damaged: one long room has been carefully restored, and a flight of steps leads to a series of dark passages in the lower storey. Near the heart of the complex is an elegant small chamber, the dome of which rested on muqarnas, preceded by a tiny vestibule with a niche of ogival form. Reused Byzantine cornices remind us that much of the material used for the construction was recycled, and in the south-eastern tower in particular it is clear that the castle itself was reinforced in successive stages. The southern stretch of the walls is partly preserved and much of the passage behind these can be followed.

Harim is not a manicured site. Tourists are few, and the police in the town may demand to see a passport. The shepherd's dog growls in disapproval; a local youth shouts from one of the openings round the well shaft, and others loiter on the walls, heedless of the weight of history that makes the place so intriguing to the foreigner, but delighting no doubt in the contrasting views, upwards to the jebel and down over the plain. Perhaps it is the proximity of the border that makes the eroded husk of the castle of Harim seem unexpectedly moving.

33. EBLA

From an archaeological perspective Ebla has proved, with Ugarit and Mari, to be one of the most significant early sites in Syria. The tell is a couple of kilometres/1 mile east of the main road, some 60 kilometres/37 miles south of Aleppo. The Italian excavations only started in 1964, but quickly yielded dramatic discoveries, including the archives of the Royal Palace. We now know that Ebla was a substantial town by about 2500 BC, trading widely – for Egyptian alabaster fragments and lapis lazuli from Afghanistan have been found on the site. The city became a considerable power. In about 2250 BC Ebla was sacked by Akkadians, only to revive between c.2150 and 2000 BC. Later she was dominated by Aleppo. The Hittites struck in 1600 and Ebla was never to recover.

The visitor now approaches across a bare landscape, brown in the winter, and is confronted by the rim of the tell that represents the walls of c.2000–1800 BC, which enclosed an area of some 50 hectares/124 acres. The earth embankment of the walls was some 60 metres/200 feet wide. A section of the stone footings of the original mud-brick superstructure is exposed by the road at the north-western corner. From here the great central mound can be seen, dominating the unexpectedly large oval space within the walls.

The ticket office is to the west of the mound. The path to this passes to the right of the stone foundations of the Lion Court of the Temple of Ishtar, which, like the nearby Western Palace, where such elements as stone orthostats and steps are in place, represents the last phase of Ebla's evolution, c.1650 BC. The excavators at Ebla were fully aware of the damage exposure causes to mud-brick structures, and have employed differing solutions. The most radical is used for the Royal Archive building high on the south-west face of the mound, intended as is explicitly stated to make the ruins 'comprehensive' to an 'increasingly diversified tourism'! The archives' proximity to a major temple and to the shrine dedicated to the cult of royal ancestors cannot be coincidental. On the top of the mound, which in the absence of tourists a quartet of irritated dogs consider their own, was the palace of the Amorite rulers.

The most visually compelling structure at Ebla is unquestionably the formidable South, or Damascus, Gate. From the south the visitor approached the projecting outer gateway, with two huge blocks at each side. Through this was reached a rectangular enclosure. At the end of this, the route turns, at an angle, into the inner gateway, the wall on the east side of which retains its complement of basalt monoliths but not, of course, their mud-brick superstructure. The passage was of five sections of equal length, widening in the second and fourth. Elements of the footing of the wall at either side can be recognized, and inside the gate there is a flight of steps.

The South Gate.

Make a point of walking along at least one section of the wall. The emptiness of the place is almost eerie, although a bus is disgorging its tribute of tourists by the ticket office. And the views over the empty landscape are not compromised by the proximity of the motorway. A shepherd boy watches his small flock near the insubstantial remains of the western fortress, and then turns with a repetitive cry: '*Messieur backsheeesh.*' There is a further small fortress, no more visually rewarding, near by at the northern angle of the enceinte. It is largely due to the Italian excavators and their exemplary labelling that despite the removal of the remarkable finds to Damascus, Aleppo and Idlib, Ebla is now so readily comprehensible to the casual visitor.

34. JERADEH AND RUWEIHA

The 'dead cities' of the Jebel Riha are as rewarding as those in the shadow of Qalaat Semaan. Lying between the Ghab, watered by the Orontes, and the desert to the east, the jebel prospered under the ordered rule of the Byzantines. In less settled times it was largely abandoned, and this explains the survival of so many late Roman and Byzantine buildings.

South of Ebla, the ground to the west of the main road south from Aleppo rises perceptibly. Some 18 kilometres/11 miles south of Seraqib, there is a turn to the right. This leads after a few kilometres to the substantial ruins of a cluster of houses, once walled, upon which the modern village of Jeradeh has encroached. Many of the houses are relatively large. There is a single church, with columns flanking the nave; but the most impressive monument is undoubtedly the tower. Taken together the ruins are rewarding not least for the way they exploit the rising ground, and certainly deserve a brief survey en route to the rather more remarkable site of Ruweiha, some 2 kilometres/1 mile or so further on.

From a distance Ruweiha dominates its landscape, and modern buildings hardly disturb the silhouette of the Byzantine settlement. The road passes a necropolis, with a most elegant tomb in the form of a small temple, with a Doric portico resting on only two columns and a sepulchral chamber behind. The centre of the town was further on. A little to the north of the road is a handsome fifth-century church of basilica type, the aisles separated from the generously proportioned nave by rows of eight columns. A number of subsidiary structures survive in the compound, which is now used by a farmer. Just over 100 metres/

Jeradeh: the tower.

109 yards to the north-east is the unexpectedly large agora, where the local tradesmen marketed their wares under a double Ionic colonnade. This was evidently the focal point of the community, which explains why the surrounding area was extensively developed.

The most ambitious monument of Ruweiha is on higher ground 250 metres/273 yards ahead. The Church of Bissos was, as the inscription on one of the two substantial tombs at either side states, built for the benefactor of that name, who asked the reader to pray for him. Bissos evidently had expansive ideas. His church was the largest in the Jebel Riha. The builder he employed was in the vanguard of church design: the nave was roofed by two great transverse arches and by arches resting on the four piers; and there are inventive horseshoe arches above the subsidiary doors on the west front. Unfortunately the transverse arches were inadequately supported and as a result much of the nave has collapsed. The stone dome of Bissos's tomb chamber is, however, intact. The whole complex was surrounded by a defensive wall. Near by there are more houses, many preserved to full height, with internal courtyards.

Reweiha in its heyday was the centre of a prosperous agricultural community. And the appeal of what survives owes much to the fact that the land is still farmed. There are small plots of cultivated ground, and animals are left to graze: a tethered donkey here, cattle there. The place is at its most magical in the late afternoon, when sunlight catches the façades of the two churches.

35. BARA

Of the numerous 'dead cities' of northern Syria, Bara, the Byzantine Kapropera, is certainly among the most remarkable. Settled in the fourth century, Bara in its fifth- and sixth-century heyday benefited from a conveniently placed and well-watered position in the valley between the two sections of the Jebel Riha, and became the largest centre in the area. While Bara can be reached from Riha to the north, is it also accessible from Maarat by way of Kfer Nabbil, 7 kilometres/4 miles away, from where the route is well marked. As the road winds through an undulating wooded valley a turn to the right may tempt you to the ruins of Shinsharah. Don't resist. The 3-kilometre/2-mile detour is rewarded by a particularly well-preserved village with two dozen sizeable houses, or rather blocks of houses, many standing to roof level. These were set in compounds, often with subsidiary buildings. The houses were of up to four sections, each for different families, and most had colonnades at ground-floor level. Often the lintels and window hoods were decorated, and the façades enriched with niches. Attached to one block is a somewhat ponderous pedimented mausoleum with angle pilasters. The site was served by cisterns and reservoirs – and of course by a church, relatively modest in size.

Returning to the main road, you pass a sign to another 'dead city', Sheila, and then skirt two more. In the first, Bekusa, there is an elegant church hard by the road. The modern town of al-Bara, strung along a ridge, is not appealing. Take the first turn to the left. Soon there is a prospect of the jagged walls of the Roman and Byzantine market town of Kapropera, caught most sharply in the morning sunlight. The road sinks to cross a wadi and then climbs up between some substantial ruined houses. Turn left, passing an elegant rock-cut mausoleum with three arches, for

The smaller pyramidal tomb.

the Deir Sobat, a substantial monastery with a large central space off which are an oratorium and other rooms. The complex has been tactfully restored.

Return past the mausoleum and turn left. Almost immediately you reach the finest monument of Byzantine Bara, the larger of the two pyramidal-roofed tombs. The massive base is richly decorated, with Corinthian pilasters at the corners and a crisp acanthus cornice. The lintel of the door on the east side is also richly carved. Within the chamber, visible through the locked grill, are five fine sarcophagi. Like the other monuments at Bara, the tomb is surrounded by small plots of tillage and by olive trees. As I lingered on my last visit, members of a family were hacking at the trees and collecting the prunings, the women as vigorously as the men. Not far to the east of the tomb is a reasonably well-preserved sixth-century church, with a fine east wall. Beside this is a smaller church. Other churches, mostly in less happy condition, and really of interest only to the elect, lie in a line to the north. More interesting to most visitors will be the smaller, but impeccably preserved, pyramidal-roofed tomb to which the road continues. The slight projections on the blocks of the roof catch the sunlight.

Turning right by the second pyramid the road descends to the valley. As the ground rises on the east side, a track to the left leads more or less in the direction of the Qalaat Abu Safian, which dominates the site from the north. This unexpectedly elegant castle, built inevitably of pillaged masonry, consisted of a keep flanked to the east and south by a bailey with three towers on the south wall and defended to the west by two further towers. Enough is visible of the upper room of the keep, a window and a section of cornice, to show that it was an Ayyubid building of considerable refinement, built or remodelled after 1123, when the Crusaders who had taken Bara in 1098 were driven out by the resurgent Muslims. The top of the tower remains the best place from which to survey the ruins of Byzantine Bara.

Qalaat Abu Safian: garderobe.

36. SERJILLA

From Bara a road to the east passes the 'dead city' of Bauda, with a fine pyramidal tomb and a scattering of houses to reach, after 7 kilometres/ 4 miles, the ruins of Serjilla. The setting is beautiful, a fold in a narrow valley that widens to the south. And here, most remarkably, a Byzantine village has survived more or less intact.

The road leads to a new car park, for Serjilla is now on the recognized tourist itinerary, the principal benefit of which is the excellent labelling. The village is spread out ahead. The main path descends past a small necropolis towards the centre of the site. The first major building is the bath complex, built in 473. The entrance was from the opposite east side. A vestibule led to the large central hall, originally with four columns at the further end. A door to the left opened to a vestibule with a footbath, from which the small apsed frigidarium, the tepidarium and the calidarium, flanking the south wall of the hall, were reached. Evidence of the sophisticated water system can be seen, and to the south there is a substantial cistern, the roof blocks of which remain in place. Beside this is an elegant structure, with a double-tiered portico of three columns to the south, formerly identified as an andron, or meeting room for men, but now thought to be an inn for pilgrims. This is remarkably well preserved, lacking little more than the wooden beams, the positions of which are indicated by the holes into which these fitted. Higher up, and to the east, is a relatively modest church which may originally have antedated the year cited in an inscription, 372, but was progressively enlarged at the period of the area's high agricultural prosperity, the fifth and sixth centuries, and may have become a place of pilgrimage.

The inn.

Above the church, on gently sloping ground, was the main residential area, with a number of sixth-century houses, many like those of Shinsharah and Bara perhaps intended for multiple occupation, with two-tiered colonnaded fronts set in walled enclosures. Most have lintels proclaiming their original builders' commitment to their faith. A fine example above the church is so well preserved that the roof trusses can be counted. Another to the south-west, the colonnade of which has largely fallen, is equally impressive in detail: parts of it are used for animals. More such houses are scattered on the western side of the valley. To the west of these is a beautiful small mausoleum, with a chaste pilastered portal and a roof of overlying slabs.

Apart from the tents above the car park, no modern structure intrudes. There are indeed few places where one feels so close to the pulse of life in a Byzantine rural community, or so aware of its quiet sophistication. What, one wonders, must the Crusaders have made of such settlements, when they came in 1098? For no comparable rural houses existed at the time in Western Europe. Fortunately other buildings were yet closer to their small outpost of Rubea, little more than a kilometre/two-thirds of a mile to the south-west, for otherwise Serjilla would doubtless have been exploited as a quarry of convenience. This was spared and comes down to us as the 'dead city' of northern Syria which it is easiest to imagine as a living entity. However little we can really hope to understand the preoccupations of the men who lived in the elegant houses, we can assume that they worried about the vagaries of the market for olive oil and grumbled at the taxes levied by their political masters.

37. MAARAT AL-NUMAN

Maarat is a sleepy town between Aleppo and Hama. In the past it was at times less tranquil. After a siege of three weeks, Maarat fell to the First Crusade in 1099: a notorious massacre ensued and Frankish troops in their own desperation resorted to cannibalism. The Crusaders were driven out by Zengi of Aleppo in 1135, and Maarat was immediately reclaimed for Islam. A handsome minaret, rebuilt after 1170, recalls that of the Great Mosque of Aleppo; and near by is the fine Madrasa Abu al-Fawaris of 1199. But ironically it is on account of an earlier Christian past that Maarat now deserves to be visited.

South-east of the centre of the town is an unusually large han built for a sixteenth-century Ottoman pasha, Murad, and intended for pilgrims on the Haj. This has been put to inspired use as a museum for a remarkable series of mosaics. The earliest, and arguably the most distinguished, was found in Homs, and is in the first section of the han on the left. Assigned to the third century, it shows incidents from the legend of Hercules, including a sophisticated rendering of the hero protecting Oceanus, the sea god, from an intimidating serpent, entwined around a tree.

The other significant mosaics all come from Byzantine churches and reflect the vigorous agricultural economy, based on the production of olive oil, which persisted in the limestone country to the west until the Arab invasion. These are not arranged chronologically. There are some fine geometrical designs, but inevitably it is the representations of animals that are most memorable. The fifth-century lion in pursuit of a gazelle from Kafr Tab is impressive in its sense of movement. Closely contemporary are the pavements from Maarat Bitar, including a nearly symmetrical group of animals and birds round a vase, and a lioness attacking a stallion.

The mosaic from Umm Galal, sixth century AD.

Gruesome in a rather different way is the scene of 449 from Umm Hartin, with two sacrificed bulls whose blood is being drunk by birds. Equally striking are the pavements of 511 from Firkiye, with Romulus and Remus being suckled by the wolf and other animals including a sheep grazing and a lion devouring its prey, in a particularly effective border of simulated ribbon. Also of the early sixth century are a series of floors from Maarat, notably a long scene subdivided by trees, in one section of which a man leads his horse by the bridle. Placed before these, no doubt for reasons of space, is the large mosaic of 567 from Hawat, with animals crowded together from either side in the main field, and an almost predictable associated scene of a lion attacking a bull.

Visitors to the bare, ruined churches in Bara and the villages near by get a very distorted view of their original character unless they have seen the mosaics at Maarat, with their subtle tonality of reds and browns. And the innumerable carved basalt doors set out in the courtyard of the han remind us that the Byzantine farmer was as aware of his need for security in this world as he was of his hope for salvation in the next.

Khan Murad Pasha.

38. HAMA

Nobly set on a triple bend of the Orontes, Hama remains a place of exceptional interest, despite the destruction of much of the ancient city in 1982. Moreover, partly because it is well supplied with hotels at every level, the city is the most convenient base for visitors to many key sites. Hama is of course best known for the nourias, the great wooden wheels used to raise water from the river: and anyone who arrives at Hama for the first time will be awed by their size.

Hama was settled as early as the Neolithic period, and excavation of the tell has elucidated successive phases of occupation. By the eleventh century BC, Hama controlled the minor kingdom of Hamath, which at differing times was in the sphere of influence of King Solomon and of Damascus. The city fell to the Assyrians in 720 BC but gradually recovered. Renamed Epiphania in honour of the Seleucid King Antiochus IV Epiphanes (175–164 BC), it continued to be of importance under Roman and Byzantine rule. Later, Hama was inevitably affected by rivalries between the rulers of Aleppo and Damascus. The victory of the Ayyubids in the twelfth century heralded a period of renewed prosperity. More recently under Ottoman rule, Hama became a redoubt of extreme Sunni conservatism.

Before examining Hama's monuments it makes sense to visit the excellent new museum north of the old town, off the Aleppo road. This is arranged chronologically, beginning with Stone Age implements. Among the early pottery is a remarkable incense burner in the form of a round tower of five sections, with three openings on each at alternating angles. The Iron Age room ranges from inscriptions in Lowian, a Hittite script, to the huge but much-reconstructed basalt lion found on the citadel of Hama, on which the details of the pelt are finely realized. There is also a smaller bewhiskered semi-lion, which originally flanked a door: look out for a photograph of this *in situ* during the Dutch excavations on the tell.

Roman Hama is represented by a statue of a woman, which most unusually retains much of the original red paint. More arresting is an exceptionally fine mosaic of third century from Mariamin, a village near by. This shows a group of young women playing musical instruments: they look like sisters, and one can well imagine the sounds they create reverberating from the floor of planks laid with nails. The Byzantine exhibits are on the whole of less distinction, but a mosaic of 469 from Apamea is of particular relevance, as it shows a nouria very like those that survive. The clou of the medieval Islamic collection is the mimbar of 1163 given by Nur al-Din to his mosque in the town: the upper section and one side of the balustrade, displayed separately, are original. The wide commercial horizons of medieval Syria are implied by fourteenth-century Syrian blue and white bowls which were inspired by Chinese prototypes.

The river was Hama's *raison d'être*. The first cluster of nourias, four in all, are to the east of the centre. The wooden wheels are inevitably recent replacements, but many of the aqueducts these serve, some with pointed arches, are medieval. Downstream, where the Orontes turns sharply northwards, two fine nourias face each other. The best-preserved section of the old city follows on the left bank, with a sequence of stone buildings, including the al-Uthmaniye Hammam, still in use, and Beit al-Azem, the elegant waterside palace of Assad Pasha al-Azem, who governed Hama before he was promoted to Damascus, where he built an even larger establishment. The palace is now a museum. From a large court with an iwan, the visitor ascends to a higher courtyard with a portico on the northern side. The impressive rooms off this have been comprehensively restored. The north wing centres on a domed cruciform hall, lavishly faced with marbles, painted stucco and wood, inset with small pieces of mirror, as well as coloured glass. The circuit continues with a small bath, and ends in a room below the loggia in a third, and smaller, court: here the painted panels and stucco have not been redone.

Beyond the palace a door beside the road opens to a further group of nourias – boys are trying with limited success to set the largest into motion. Further on, a vaulted passage flanks the mosque of Nur al-Din. This was begun in 1172. The minaret of black basalt and yellowish limestone is particularly elegant, and there is a beautiful appropriated Corinthian capital in the courtyard. A little way to the west of the mosque is the southern end of the tell of the early settlement. The summit of this is laid out as a park, and the depression left by the excavations is visible. No one who lingers to hear the orchestrated call to prayer will be left in any doubt of Hama's continuing Sunni orthodoxy.

Downstream from the tell there are more nourias. The largest is on the left bank: an inscription on its high aqueduct of 1361 establishes that the water was intended to serve the Great Mosque, which is reached by a street that runs to the west from the southern end of the tell. The mosque was partly destroyed in 1982, but has been reconstituted with considerable success, using much of the original fabric. The minarets have been convincingly rebuilt and the great courtyard with its treasury raised on six ancient columns is in no sense a pastiche. The ancient blocks on the south wall of the prayer hall have been carefully put back in place. At the south-western corner there is a vestibule with more recycled blocks, four sharply carved Byzantine brackets and a handsome Roman lintel with an acanthus frieze.

There are several other early mosques in Hama, and small sections of the early city survive on both sides of the river. The modern souks are mostly concentrated to the north-west of al-Marabut Street, which runs south-west of the central duo of nourias and is dignified by two substantial Ottoman khans, respectively of 1556 and 1738.

Nourias on the Orontes.

39. QASR IBN WARDAN

In Hama, where the groaning of the nourias on the Orontes can at times still be heard, it is easy to forget how close one is to the fringe of the undulating desert that stretches towards the Euphrates, a fringe that man has tamed in the past and upon which modern development now encroaches. In Byzantine times this terrain supported a substantial population. And only this can explain the scale of the ruins at Qasr Ibn Wardan, some 60 kilometres/37 miles to the north-east. The road passes a number of settlements, some with decaying beehive buildings of the type that is so characteristic of the area and is found as far to the north as Harran across the Turkish border.

The main portal: detail.

The buildings, looming in the morning sun, are on a low elevation west of the modern village. Two, the palace and the church to the west of this, stand to full height. To the south

The gallery of the church.

of the former was a substantial quadrangular barrack block of which only stumps survive. All three were built in 561–4, at the end of the reign of the Emperor Justinian, evidently as part of a programme to reinforce Syria as a bulwark against Sasanian aggression from the east.

The palace is roughly 50 metres/160 feet square. The south front was intended to impress those who arrived from the direction of Hama, and was evidently designed by an architect with an informed knowledge of contemporary developments at Byzantium. The masons followed the metropolitan practice of using alternating bands of stone and brick, here predominantly with three courses of relatively small basalt blocks and ten of thin bricks. The central doorway, flanked by jambs decorated with trailing fronds, leads to an atrium with coved ends, opening to apsed rooms at either side, from which further chambers are reached. A stair to the left of the room on the right mounts to a spectacular cross-shaped gallery above. Most of the vault of this has fallen, but some of the original plaster survives; and there are early Muslim graffiti, including small outlines of animals. The west wing stands in part to first-floor level and has an unexpectedly generous staircase. The ruins of the north and eastern ranges are less substantial.

The church, although not large, was of unusual sophistication and also is more metropolitan than local in character. The west door led to a narrow narthex, and thus to the apsed nave, which was separated by pairs of columns from the lateral aisles that linked with the ends of the narthex. Stairs in a tower at the north-west corner lead to elegantly arcaded galleries, of which that on the north is intact. The brick dome, now largely fallen, was supported by the lateral walls.

The recent restoration of both buildings has been admirably tactful; and as there is now an official guardian the visitor can be reasonably confident of gaining admittance.

40. ANDERIN

Anyone who visits Qasr Ibn Wardan should go on to Anderin, the Byzantine Androna. An excellent road north-eastwards passes a sequence of desert villages, one with an evocative group of beehive houses, and after 20 kilometres/12½ miles there is an inadequately marked turn to the right.

The first impression after the more or less level desert is of an undulating expanse, green only in the low depressions, contained within a dyke that represents the very extensive circuit of the walls of stone, which were reinforced by towers. The only obvious building in sight is the broken arch of the apse of the cathedral, nearly a kilometre/two-thirds of a mile away. Rather than charge on to this, follow the track within the walls to the left. Public buildings apart, the structures of Anderin were of mud brick on stone foundations and, sometimes, with stone doors. Among the humps of earth pairs of door jambs appear. Beside a number of these are fallen lintels, some with inscribed crosses and the letters alpha and omega. The wind restrains the heat of the sun. An owl perches on a lintel. A lizard scuttles back into its burrow. Underfoot the soil is littered with shards, among which the odd fragment of glass catches the sunlight, and with bits of the characteristic grooved Byzantine tiles.

The West Gate has recently been partly exhumed from the debris, its paving rutted by ancient wheels. Making towards a group of four door jambs, you pass a cistern and then see another recent excavation: a building of some size, with, near by, a substantial cistern whose roof of basalt blocks was supported on two arches. Near the East Gate there is another building, the lintel of whose southern gate survives in fragments. But it is time to make for the skeleton of the cathedral. This was built both of stone and of brick, slumped sections of which remain where

A fallen lintel.

they fell. The cathedral was of rather ambitious size, for Androna had a sizeable population, to judge both from the large area within its walls and from the considerable number of churches reported a century ago by the indefatigable Professor Butler of Princeton University.

Near the cathedral, and at the heart of the town, where its two main arteries crossed, is the most impressive building at Anderin. The barrack complex, which has recently been cleared of sand, is comparable with Qasr Ibn Wardan, both in apparent function and in its use of alternating bands of basalt blocks and brick. There is a fine entrance on the east, decorated with stylized plants. The west door, set back, is even more distinguished. This opens to an atrium. To the right there is a ramp, two sections of which survive, rather than a staircase; ahead are the fallen columns and lintel of the west front of a substantial apsed church. To the west of the complex is a building that was as essential to a Byzantine as to a Roman garrison, the baths, equipped inevitably with such amenities as a hypocaust. On the north side the building had a short colonnade.

Part of the charm of Anderin is that it is still little known, although on my more recent visit an appreciative local family were inspecting the cathedral. Many of the secrets of ancient Androna remain to be discovered, but nonetheless one is awed by the Byzantines' ability to plant so considerable a town in so uncompromising a terrain. Their loss of Syria led to a gradual abandonment of the place. There is a small modern settlement to the north, but happily this seems wholly insignificant against the immeasurable expanse of level semi-desert that stretches in every direction.

41. ISRIYA

I first met the elegant Roman temple at Isriya in an old photograph at the Baron Hotel; but Mr Mazloumian was absolutely certain that my car would not get me there. Some years later with a day in hand and hoping that an ordinary motor could manage 30 kilometres/19 miles for which Burns considered four-wheel drive 'advisable', on a track along the pipeline that passes the site, I set out from Hama. To my amazement a new and absolutely empty tarmac road stretched out ahead, and so what had seemed something of challenge was nothing of the kind.

For the Romans, Seriana was a key junction on the roads from Emesa (Homs) and Salaminias (Selemiye) to Resafe and the Euphrates, and from Palmyra to the military stronghold of Chalcis (Qinnesrin) and thence to Antioch. The position of the town was carefully chosen, on the lower northern slopes of a ridge that erupts from the more or less level semi-desert, which reaches to the horizon. The temple stands on a rise, above what is now a graveyard. The whitish limestone has been burnished to a pale yellow by exposure except where blown sand has protected the lower section of the walls. The upper blocks have been eroded by the wind. The portico has gone. But otherwise the building is impressively complete. The door, which faces east, is finely decorated, and was given structural protection by a relieving arch above. But it is the disciplined use of shallow pilasters on the outer walls that makes the temple so memorable, breaking what would otherwise be the monotony of sun-struck surfaces with subtle shadows. The capitals, of which some are reasonably well preserved, are Corinthian. There is no caretaker at Isriya, but it is possible to squeeze under the metal door to enter the cella

The temple, from the north-west.

and climb the spiral stairs in the corner to the right of the entrance.

Isriya's remote situation no doubt adds to its fascination; but now that the Syrian authorities have done so much to reverse the process of desertification, and greatly extended the road system, it is much more practical to plan a visit in conjunction with other sites. A perfectly good road from Qasr Ibn Wardan reaches after 50 kilometres/31 miles the new highway as it approaches Isriya: signs are non-existent, but keep to the same general line at the numerous junctions. If you visit Isriya on a circuit from Hama, you may want on the way back to take in Qalaat al-Shmemis, west of Selimiye, crowning a long extinct volcano which it is impossible not to see from afar. The castle was part of the Ayyubid outer defence of Hama, built in the thirteenth century by the governor, Assad al-Din Shirkoh. The moat is impressive. But the castle itself is in a parlous state, tottering on the black basalt tip of the almost white cone.

There is a tempting alternative. A sign at Isriya to Khanazir, the ancient Anasarthon, and Aleppo means that another Roman route now can be followed, taking in the Byzantine sites in the desert between Khanazir and Sfire south of Aleppo. South of Khanazir the road passes what must be one of the largest extant clusters of beehive houses.

42. MASYAF

A mere 37 kilometres/23 miles west of Hama, the castle of Masyaf visibly belonged to a very different world. To the impeccably Sunni Ayyubids the Ismaelis, who revered Ismael, a son of the sixth Shi'ite imam, were anything but desirable neighbours. By the late eleventh century their sect controlled many of the valleys of the Elburz Mountains in Persia. The support of Ridwan of Aleppo enabled them to begin to build up a position in Syria, and they came to control much of the Jebel Ansariye, assiduously playing off the Crusaders, who held the coastal strip to the west of the mountains, and the Sunni rulers of Aleppo and Damascus. Widely known as the Assassins, from their exploitation of hashish to enhance the performance of those selected to dispatch their enemies, they would no doubt be gratified by the survival of their name in connection with the political murders they conducted with such efficiency.

Masyaf is both the most accessible and the best preserved of the castles of the Assassins in Syria. It crests a spur of rock to the east of the town. Recycled material in the walls demonstrates that the site was fortified at least from the Seleucid period. In 1103 this fell to the Crusaders, as they sought to extend their territory eastwards. By 1140–1 it was in the hands of the Ismaelis. The most easterly of their Syrian fortresses, Masyaf became a place of much importance to them. The Assassins were at their zenith under Rashid al-Din Sinan, known by the Crusaders as 'The Old Man of the Mountain', who was sent from Iran in 1162 and ruled from 1163 until his death thirty years later. When Saladin had the temerity to lay siege to Masyaf in 1176, Sinan arranged for a dagger with a menacing poem and cakes that were still warm to be placed on his bed. The massage was taken, and the Ismaelis retained their territory for a further century.

The castle is at its most impressive from the east, particularly when clouds have gathered over the jebel and the sunlight comes and goes. The wall is flanked by numerous square towers, and rises above the rough flanks of the bedrock, which are some 10 metres/33 feet high. The Ismaelis exploited what they found and traces of the regular ashlar masonry so characteristic of the Crusaders can be seen. But at Masyaf what is striking is the Assassins' use of small irregular pieces of stone. As astute a judge as Saladin would not have underrated the effectiveness of the defences.

Many fortresses are most impressive from outside and this is most emphatically true of Masyaf. The entrance is at the south, through a vaulted passage, near which is an arch rising from Byzantine capitals. There are the inevitable cisterns and numerous storerooms, as well as some more ambitious rooms behind the wall to the east.

The town of Masyaf has relatively little to commend it. The sightseer bound for Hama may, however, be tempted to make a detour to the two churches at Deir Soleib, reached from a side road 10 kilometres/ 6 miles east of Masyaf. The West Church, a kilometre/two-thirds of a mile before the village, is particularly rewarding, and the valley has an unusual charm. Nowhere have I seen anemones in more carpeted profusion. However, the castle lover will take the road north from Masyaf and make for the Assassins' castle of Abu Qobeis, high above the flank of the Jebel Ansariye. The ruins are not particularly distinguished, but the view down over the Ghab, the plain watered by the Orontes, and across to the great fortress of Shaizar is unforgettable.

The castle, from the east.

43. SHAIZAR

North-west of Hama, the Orontes carves through a curving gorge to reach a wide valley, the Ghab, which stretches northwards. The modest modern town of Shaizar lies below a tapering ridge, some 300 metres/328 yards long, which was first fortified by the Fatimids. The Byzantines took this is 999; but in 1081 it fell to the Banu Munqidhs, the memoirs of one of whom, Usamah Ibn Munqidh, are an invaluable record of the age of the Crusades from a Muslim perspective, with accounts of hunting and of battles and of a Christian knight deciding to be shaved in the local fashion at a hammam in Hama. In 1108 and again in 1110 Shaizar defied Tancred of Antioch; for half a century it was to be in the front line of resistance to Crusader expansion. After an earthquake of 1157, the Crusaders finally seized part of the castle, but they proved to be no match for the forces of Nur al-Din. The defences of Shaizar were reinforced by the Ayyubids and, after the destructive Mongolian incursion of 1260, by the Mameluke Sultan Baibars and his heir, Sultan Qalaun. In more settled times, Shaizar lost its military importance. Eventually a village grew up within the walls, only to be expelled in 1958, when the historic interest of the ruins came to be recognized. Recently a programme of clearance and restoration has been undertaken with Italian assistance.

The castle is approached from the northern tip. A reconstructed bridge rises to a handsome entrance tower, built in several stages, but completed in 1290, as an inscription attests. The tower is constructed of finely rusticated blocks, and bonded with recycled column drums. The earlier section to the right, above a handsome late twelfth-century glacis, is built to a pronounced batter. From the gate, a wide passage, partly cut into the rock, leads upwards to the long enclosure, while a steeper and narrower one rises after two sharp bends to a corridor that gave access

A nouria under repair.

to the fortifications above the gate; after the covered section beyond the turning to a further passage climbing to the right, an inscription spans the arch of a second vault. As the ridge rises there is the surviving outer section of a fine Ayyubid tower of excellent rusticated ashlar blocks with rooms on two floors. This hangs over the precipitous rise from the river: the outer angles are canted to accommodate arrow slits that could command the ground at either side.

Most of the other structures towards the centre of the fortress are of lesser interest. Some are relatively modern and others are in precarious condition. Cisterns abound. At the furthest point is the most handsome keep. In the past this could only be entered by the agile, but now it has been restored. The section on the right, of relatively coarse masonry, is of after 1157; that in the centre, again in flat rusticated masonry, was built in 1233, under the Ayyubid al-Malik al-Aziz, as the impressive inscription proclaims, while the eastern part, which breaks forward, is of later in the thirteenth century. One cannot but be struck by the splendour of the position, looking down to the great bend of the Orontes, although this is now, alas, disfigured by ill-sited development to the south and smoke rising from a nearby factory. The most memorable view of the keep itself is, however, from the tremendous rock-cut ditch, which cut off the fortress from the higher ground to the south. This can be reached from a road along the west side of the ridge.

To the north of the castle is a well-restored early bridge with eleven arches. Downstream, at either side of the river and served by a well-maintained weir that deflects water to them, there are nourias, perhaps on the sites of medieval predecessors. Both are still in use. On a recent visit men were laboriously replacing rotten timbers in what was clearly the time-honoured way.

44. APAMEA

Apamea is the phoenix among the classical cities of Syria. Despite the advantages of its situation above the productive agricultural land of the Ghab in an area of good grazing, the city was abandoned in the Middle Ages. Early travellers found the place unrewarding, but as a result of excavations initiated by the Belgians in 1930 and the more recent work of the Syrian authorities no one who now visits Apamea can be disappointed.

With Antioch, its port of Seleucia and Latakia, Apamea was one of four major cities founded by Alexander the Great's successor in the area, Seleucus I Nicator. The city proper occupied a roughly oblong area high on the eastern flank of the valley, reasonably protected by the fall of the ground on the other sides, and by a detached conical hill on the west that rises sheer from the valley floor and lent itself for defence. Pompey secured the area for Rome in 64 BC. A major earthquake on 13 December AD 115 necessitated an ambitious programme of reconstruction in which the Emperor Trajan clearly took an interest. The city continued to be a significant economic centre, served by numerous churches and a synagogue. Early in the fifth century Apamea became the capital of Syria Secunda. The city was sacked by Khoesroe I of Persia in 540 and never fully recovered. Byzantine rule of the area was broken by the Persians in 573 and in 612–28, and ended abruptly in the aftermath of the Battle of the Yarmuk in 636, no doubt to the relief of the local Christians whose Monophysite convictions the Byzantines had sought to suppress.

The citadel, Qalaat al-Mudiq, remained in use. This fell to Tancred of Antioch in 1106, but was recovered by Nur al-Din in 1149. Eight years later an earthquake shattered what survived of the city. A village developed within the citadel and the Ottomans were to build both a mosque and a caravanserai for pilgrims on the Haj below this.

The citadel hangs above the road, its walls, partly patched under the Mamelukes, not unimpressive from afar. The village within these is a bustling place, and of the few points at which the visitor can get to the walls the most rewarding is a tower on the east side, with a room flanked by paired arches that does service as a cowshed. Wandering through the narrow streets one comes across the occasional column drum.

Roads at either side of the citadel climb up to the plateau, which is crested by the city walls, over 10 kilometres/6 miles in circumference. Resist the temptation to take the road that cuts to the centre, where the cardo and decumanus intersect, and turn north below the majestic line of the walls, which were strengthened with square towers under Justinian. These can be followed by road almost as far as the site of the South Gate. Then return to the North Gate, which also was reinforced by the Byzantines, and leads to the remarkable portico-lined cardo, which is the most striking feature of Apamea.

The Romans saw the earthquake of 115 as a challenge, and the reconstruction of the northern section of the Seleucid plateia as the cardo was completed in 117. The elegant Corinthian columns of the first section support an entablature of equal refinement. The cardo was laid out in four campaigns, marked by votive columns at the first and second major intersections, and by the junction with the main decumanus. Walking along the street, one is quickly conscious of changes in detail, in the scale of the column drums, in the extent of the fluting, in the occasional use of decorated sections above the bases, in the addition of brackets for statues – as at Palmyra – and, not least, in the employment of spiral fluting, some alternating in direction – an eastern departure from the rigid classical canon as expressed by Vitruvius. In some places the original paving has been revealed, and the odd game board can be seen

The cardo.

cut into these. There is evidence of a sophisticated drainage system. The porticoes were backed by shop fronts, parts of some of which stand. The excavators found stretches of the long mosaic of animals which lay behind some of the columns: these are now in Brussels, where they are set behind a reconstruction of the wonderful row of spirally fluted columns of AD 168 on the left – east – side of the street, just after the second votive column and opposite the Temple of Tyche, or Tycheion. There are buildings to see at either hand, Trajan's Baths before the first votive column and the agora behind the Tycheion. But it is the double colonnade that mesmerizes, here virtually intact, there completely gone. The light shifts as the clouds pass; and the eye is drawn to the citadel to the west, and to the hills of the Jebel Ansariye beyond.

The intersection with the decumanus is marked now by a ticket office and restaurant. Go on to the end of the cardo, which peters out where the ground falls away to the south. Then wander back. On the east of the cardo is the Atrium Church, enlarged under Justinian and overlying an earlier synagogue, the patterned mosaics of 391 from which are now at Brussels. Opposite, near the main crossroads, are the footings of an ambitious round church, also of Justinian's time.

At the intersection follow the decumanus to the Eastern Gate. After some 300 metres/328 yards there is a substantial complex on higher ground to the right. This, it has been suggested, was the palace of the governor responsible for the province of Syria Secunda. The exceptional hunting mosaic found here, now in Brussels, is certainly of fully metropolitan calibre. Below the palace is the Eastern Cathedral, still partly filled with collapsed brickwork from the vault. On the opposite side of the decumanus is one of the most attractive buildings at Apamea, the House of the Consoles, with an entrance door, the lintel of which is supported on scrolls, and a most elegant peristyle. By the time I got there on my most recent visit, I had long since disappointed the would-be vendors of antiquities, real and false, who charge round the site on scooters, and was of no interest to a group of youths who were egging a fearless exhibitionist to demonstrate his athletic skills on a motorcycle.

The colonnaded cardo of Apamea was among the longest in the Roman Empire. The theatre, built into the flank of the hill south-east of the citadel, was also of exceptional size. Long exploited as a quarry, it is a convenient pausing place on the way down to the Ottoman caravanserai in the centre of the modern town. This is of an unusual scale, with a vast courtyard surrounding a deep cistern reached by a broad flight of steps. The cavernous halls lend themselves admirably to the display of mosaics, although dust is an inevitable problem. The circuit starts on the left. In the first room is a remarkable composition of *Socrates and the Sages* from the building that preceded the Eastern Cathedral: this dates from 362–3 during the brief reign of Julian the Apostate and, despite its ostensible expression of pre-Christian beliefs, reflects the iconography of the early church. Not dissimilar in style and from the same source is the *Judgement of the Nereids* near by.

Fifth-century mosaics have been brought from other churches in the area, notably those at Huarte. These include an impressive *Adam Naming the Animals* and a scene with a large package borne on bars slung between two donkeys, of which that in front is led by a man, both of 487, in addition to numerous representations of the violent animal combats of which there was so strong a local tradition. Among the smaller fragments, one with three fish is unusually effective. That so many mosaics have been found in the area reminds us that Apamea was the main city in one of the most prosperous regions of Byzantine Syria.

45. QALAAT BURZEY

Whatever we may now think of the mixed motives of the Crusaders, their energy and dynamism cannot fail to impress. In architectural terms Burzey is not to be thought of as a competitor to Saone or Margat or Krak, not least for the compelling reason that so little of the fabric survives. But the setting is incomparable. 'If I had to pick a spot to build a Frankish castle,' Burns observes, 'this would be it.' Although the site can be made out from Apamea, it is still relatively inaccessible. From Apamea, take the main road north to Jisr ash Shughur, which crosses the Ghab and then runs at the foot of the Jebel Ansariye. Thirty-eight kilometres/ 24 miles from Apamea, and 2.5 kilometres/1½ miles beyond the junction with a road across the massif from Latakia, the castle can be seen on a spur of rock hanging from the lower tier of the jebel. The route is fairly obvious, but the ground is rough and in summer the going would be uncomfortably warm: despite taking too precipitous a path at one stage, I took forty minutes.

In classical times Burzey was known as Lysias. It was in the hands of a Jewish leader when Pompey descended on Syria in 64 BC; and the Byzantines with their eye to strategic possibilities refortified it. Burzey was probably taken by the Crusaders in 1103, as Tancred closed in on Latakia. The castle was evidently constructed in the ensuing period and became a key outpost, controlling the approach to the jebel from the east. It fell to Saladin in August 1188, during the lightning campaign that swept away so much of the Crusaders' territory and inspired the Third Crusade.

The spur is separated by precipitous gullies from the rising hills behind. Take the valley to the north and then walk up to the site of the original

Qalaat Burzey.

entrance on the relatively exposed western side, where the curtain wall was originally protected by a glacis and by five towers. The gate tower was set within a re-entrant of the wall. Above this, to the left, on a knob of slightly higher ground, was the rectangular donjon with angle turrets. Something of the curtain wall can be traced above the steep slope to the north; on the less precipitous western section of the south side this was backed by a second wall at a higher level. But it is not just for the crumbling walls and eroded towers that one has come. Burzey was important to the Crusaders, as it enabled them to monitor movements in the Ghab, which lay at their feet. They could see the Arab successor of the citadel of Apamea – the colonnaded street of which can be descried with field glasses – and, beyond this, in the far distance, Shaizar. So can we.

One can still imagine the challenge the fortress offered Saladin when he invested it on 20 August 1188, less than a month after taking Saone, and thus cutting off Burzey from the coast. The ground to the west of the castle was some 30 metres/100 feet below this, so Saladin's mangonels could not be brought to bear. He separated his forces into three divisions and launched them in successive waves on 23 August. The first was beaten off and the second in retreat when Saladin called in the third. The western wall was breached and the heavily armed Crusaders, drained by the heat of the Syrian summer, fell back, but in such confusion that the Saracens mingled with them as they withdrew to the keep. What remained of the garrison surrendered, and Saladin promptly liberated his most glamorous captive, Sibylla, wife of the lord of Burzey and sister-in-law of Bohemond III of Antioch.

Nothing now disturbs the silence and serenity of Burzey. Unexpectedly moved, I made my way to the shattered watchtower at the north-eastern extremity of the walls, and then set off down the slope that drops precipitously towards the plain.

46. BAKAS AND SHUGHUR

Burzey was one of a number of Crusader fortresses in the hills to the west of the Orontes. It monitored the southern approach to the important bridge across the river at Jisr ash Shughur. The town itself has little of interest, but is the logical place from which to visit the twin Crusader castles of Bakas and Shughur. Six and a half kilometres/4 miles from the centre of the town, a turn to the right off the highway to Latakia leads after just over 4 kilometres/2½ miles to the village of Shughur Qadim. On the descent it is easy to make out the deep gash in the high promontory to the east that was excavated by the Crusaders as the dry moat of the southernmost castle, Bakas. This is separated from the lower fortress, Shughur, by a natural depression defended by two narrow ditches.

Between the village and the castles there is a deep ravine. The energetic will cross this and make for the great ditch, the sides of which were carefully quarried. Parts of the wall above it survive. The masonry of the eastern tower is of particularly fine quality, and is best seen from the ditch. After seeing this, return to the west side to clamber up to what remains of Bakas, a scattering of eroded walls. But it is not just for the scant ruins that one comes. On its eastern side the ridge falls abruptly to the Nahr al-Abiad, which turns majestically away just below the ditch, to flow eastwards to join the Orontes. There are few wilder prospects in Syria. The ground narrows as it descends to the north. Shughur, which had originally been fortified by the Byzantines, is no more than 30 metres/98 feet wide, but of very much greater length. Care needs to be taken, as there are a number of open cisterns. An easier but longer path to the village can be found near the gap between the two fortresses.

There is no clear evidence as to when the Crusaders built Bakas, but it

Mameluke inscription.

was clearly regarded as a significant outpost of the principality of Antioch. It ensured control of a remote yet strategically important area and, as the narrow railway near by reminds us, of a route through the hills. Saladin understood its importance. Saone fell on 30 July 1188, and Bakas followed on 5 August. The defenders withdrew to Shughur, only to surrender a week later, when it was clear that Bohemund III of Antioch was in no position to relieve them. The Crusaders were not to return. In about 1260 the Mongols occupied the castles, only to be driven out by Sultan Baibars. A beautiful inscription may be of his time. But with the fall of the Crusader kingdom Bakas lost its strategic relevance; and an earthquake of 1404 destroyed much of what survived.

47. QALAAT SALADIN: SAONE

If Krak des Chevaliers is the greatest of Crusader castles and Margat the most majestically placed, Saone is their equal in architectural interest and surpasses both in the beauty of its setting. The Jebel Ansariye falls away to the coast as a series of ridges separated by narrow valleys. And however familiar the route from Latakia or that which cuts across the grain of the hills from the nearest point on the main road to Latakia, from Jisr ash Shughar, Saone always comes as something of a surprise.

The long cliff-protected promontory that was first fortified by the Phoenicians hangs above ravines between higher ridges. The ridge falls away gradually to the west, and the gleam of the sea can be seen in the distance. Late in the tenth century the Byzantines, recognizing that the position held the key to the defence of the hinterland of Latakia, constructed what was by any standard one of the most ingenious strongholds of the time. This fell to the Crusaders early in the twelfth century, and was held in 1119 by a well-endowed feudatory of the Prince of Antioch, Robert of Saone. He and his descendants transformed the castle, building on a scale that must have seemed almost prodigal to many of their fellow barons. Their endeavours were not entirely well placed. A year after his decisive victory at Hattin, Saladin moved against the Crusader positions in northern Syria. Latakia capitulated on 23 July 1188. Four days later Saone was under siege. Saladin was ably supported by his son al-Zaher Ghazi of Aleppo, the greatest Arab castle-builder of the age, who must quickly have recognized the weakness of the lower section of the fortress. After two days the walls were breached by his mangonels, and the defenders had little alternative but to surrender.

The first sight of Saone, with the lower court at one's feet, is unforgettable, although new buildings near the village of Hafeh have rashly been allowed to take advantage of it. The road plunges to cross the deep wadi; and then climbs up below the cliffs to reach the north end of the prodigious cutting, up to 28 metres/92 feet deep, originally excavated by the Byzantines but apparently extended by the Crusaders, to protect the fortress from the gently rising ground to the east. A great square pillar of rock was left in place to support the drawbridge to a gateway. One would give much to have seen the cutting before the road through it was sealed. But there is something mesmerizing about the sheer sides, and one can see marks left by the tools of the workmen who dug and in the process quarried much of the material that was necessary for the fortress. From below, the magnificent bossed masonry of the towers seems to grow from the bedrock, but the best views of the eastern wall of the castle are to be had from the opposite side of the cutting, which is easily reachable from the south. Off centre to the right is the formidable Crusader donjon, with to the north the postern gate and on the left a stretch of wall with three round towers, originally Byzantine but refaced by the Franks.

The rock-cut pinnacle for the drawbridge.

The third of the round towers is at the angle with the south-eastern section of the wall, which the Crusaders defended with three substantial rectangular towers. The main entrance is tucked into the further, west, side of the third of these, reached by a steep path. It leads to an entrance hall opening to the north. Resist the temptation to explore the buildings on the higher ground near by and follow the line of the wall to the two other rectangular towers, the nearer of which had a well-disguised sally port. Between the next tower and that at the corner is a substantial cistern. Immediately to the north of this is the vast and gloomy stable, supported on piers.

The great donjon follows. The building admirably expresses its purpose. The walls are some 5 metres/16 feet thick. The doorway is unadorned. And the great hall on the first floor, with a groined vault some 11 metres/36 feet high resting on the massive central pier, received light only from the narrow arrow slits. The stair in the north wall gives access to a second hall, lit by three windows. A further flight mounts to the parapet, from where the plan of the upper court of the castle can most easily be read.

The Crusaders retained much of the Byzantine structure of the wall above the cliffs to the north, but they constructed two large cisterns within these. Further on, at the highest point of the site, are the remnants of the Byzantines' citadel. Below this, to the south, are a small Byzantine chapel and what survives of the Crusaders' church. To the west, before the ground falls away, there are traces of the wall between the upper and lower sections of the fortress, and of the ditch that protected it. Few visitors have time for the lower courtyard, which stretches for some 500 metres/one-third of a mile. But, particularly in spring, when the flowers are at their best, this has a magic of its own. The walls are not well preserved, but it is interesting to note how the several small square towers reinforced these at vulnerable angles and defended the two postern gates, one at either side. At the narrowest point there is an appealing Byzantine chapel, and at the extremity a much ruined Byzantine round tower.

Saladin's victory marked the end of Frankish Saone, and thus ironically enough made possible its survival as the most sophisticated extant

The donjon, from the west.

Crusader castle of the twelfth century. The place passed to a trusted Arab family, who made it over to Sultan Baibars in 1272. Later it fell to a rebellious former governor of Damascus, only to be taken by Sultan Qalaun in 1287. The palace above the entrance tower is notable for its bath complex with an elegantly carved portal, evidently constructed under the Ayyubids. By contrast the mosque near by was probably built in Qalaun's time. Ironically the Sultan's success in eliminating the Crusader strongholds on the coast by 1291 meant that the castle soon lost any strategic purpose. A village survived for some centuries in the lower courtyard, but Saone itself was abandoned to the elements.

The south-east tower.

48. UGARIT

Latakia has been a significant port since the time of the Seleucids and preserves much of their Hippodamian grid plan. But the busy modern city makes few concessions to the sightseer, despite the quality of the extant Roman tetraporticus. Long before Latakia came to prominence, a small harbour at Minet al-Beida, some 15 kilometres/9½ miles to the north, had served one of the major trading centres of the Bronze Age, the nearby town of Ugarit. The large tell, which was known in Arabic as Ras Shamra (headland of fennel), has since 1929 been systematically excavated. Major finds were divided between the Louvre and the museums of Damascus and Aleppo; and although Ugarit is perhaps visually less rewarding than Mari or Ebla it is nonetheless a place of enormous interest.

The lowest level of the tell yielded material of the seventh millennium BC. The city developed in the fourth and third millennia, but went into a sharp decline in about 2000 BC. Amorites, Canaanites of Semitic stock, migrated to Ugarit and became the majority in the ensuing period. Ugarit's resurgence owed much to them, and to the links their kings and merchants furthered with Egypt and Mesopotamia, as well as with Crete. Decline once again set in, to be reversed in the Late Bronze Age, after about 1600 BC. A devastating earthquake of 1365 BC necessitated a major reconstruction. This preceded a phase of high prosperity, made possible by a sustained peace between Egypt and the neighbouring kingdom of Mittani. It is to this period that the celebrated alphabet found at Ugarit belonged; and substantial archives discovered there mean that we know much about the life of the city. But political equilibrium was already threatened by the rise of the Hittites in Anatolia, and Ugarit's sophisticated polity could not survive the consequences of population changes and the advent of the 'Sea People' in about 1200 BC.

Ugarit: bossed masonry.

Many of those who are disgorged from the tourist buses will be puzzled by what they see. The tell is substantial. Much of what can be seen dates from Ugarit's final period. To the right of the site entrance are the not unimpressive ruins of a section of the town walls. When these were laid out, the ground in front was cut away at an angle of forty-five degrees and faced with a glacis: a small section of this survives near a reasonably well-preserved postern gate.

Above this gate is reached the entrance of the very extensive palace, the scale of which leaves us in no doubt of the sophistication of the monarchy it served. The entrance leads to the main courtyard, which was paved. The archives were kept in a room to the left of this. There are four further courts and numerous rooms, as well as traces of stairways leading to the upper storeys, now of course lost. To the north of the courtyard in the northern section of the palace is a sequence of five burial chambers, revealing a mastery of the technique of corbelling. At the eastern end of the compound was the garden, where fragments of ivory furniture were found.

Much of the tell has now been dug. Little remains of many of the buildings, but their very number suggests how claustrophobic life in a Bronze Age city would have been. Do not miss the House of Repanu, roughly on a line between the entrance to the palace and the acropolis, with a fine corbelled tomb and a circular subterranean chamber. There are other tombs under private houses in the excavated residential areas. The so-called acropolis is to the east of the tell on higher ground. Here were temples to both Baal and Dagon. What survives of the former is not unimpressive. Yet, at least in spring, when the hillside is lush and green, the setting is quite as memorable as what the archaeologists have so painstakingly unearthed and consolidated.

49. JEBLE

Jeble is an unpretending market town, now hemmed in between the coastal motorway and the shore. First mentioned in Assyrian control, Jeble was colonized at an early date by Greeks, who evidently arrived by sea. As a port the place was almost inevitably drawn into the sphere of the Phoenicians of Arwad. Later the Seleucids favoured the port's northern rival, Latakia. With Pompey's campaign of 64 BC, Jeble fell to Rome. A long period of prosperity followed.

The Roman theatre in the heart of the modern conurbation is the monument of Jeble. The position of the town on level ground meant that the Roman engineers could not take advantage of a concave hillside and thus had to build the complete structure. Seating some seven thousand, this was comparable in scale with the very much better preserved theatre at Bosra. The lower eleven rows of seats are virtually intact, as is much of the second tier of eleven rows, but only a small portion of the upper section survives. As impressive as the seating are the arched passages within the structure. Much fallen masonry can be seen and elements of the stage building can be identified.

That so much of the theatre stands must be due in part to the Crusaders. In 1198 the town surrendered to that romantic figure Raymond de Saint-Gilles, Count of Toulouse, who allowed the former ruler to retain it as tributary. Eleven years later it was annexed to Tancred's principality of Antioch, as Zibel – a name not to be confused with that of another port, Jebail, in what is now the Lebanon. The Crusaders then took the sensible course of using the theatre as the core of a fortress, as the Ayyubids did at more or less the same time at Bosra.

Crusader Zibel once again became, as it had been under the Byzantines, the seat of a bishop. It fell to Saladin on his whirlwind campaign of 1188, but was recovered by the Crusaders. In 1207 it was made over to the Knights Hospitallers, whose great stronghold of Margat is only 25 kilometres/15 miles to the south. Their control was strongly contested by the rivals, the Knights Templar. Jebel thus experienced in microcosm the riven jealousy between the two orders that fatally undermined the kingdom of Jerusalem, and no doubt assisted Sultan Qalaun in his campaign to mop up the Crusader strongholds in northern Syria. He took Jeble in 1285.

Of the Crusader cathedral no trace survives. The much-reconstructed main mosque, known for the tomb of Sidi Ibrahim Ben Adham, who died in 778, presumably took its place on the site of a substantial church erected for the ill-fated Emperor Heraclius in the seventh century. The curious can find bits of old masonry in the largely redeveloped area of the souks.

The theatre.

50. QALAAT MARQAB: MARGAT

South of Jeble the coastal plain closes in and an arm of the Jebel Ansariye stretches out towards the shore. The great castle of Marqab, the Crusader's Margat, proud on a volcanic cone, overlooks the port of Baniyas and controlled the key route from Cilicia and Antioch to Jerusalem. Margat still dominates its hinterland, a looming presence of black basalt, frowning above the green terraces of the hillsides.

While Baniyas was a Phoenician settlement, the strategic potential of the site was not recognized until 1062, when a relatively modest fortress was constructed. This fell to the Byzantines in 1104, during the aftermath of the First Crusade. Later – and certainly before 1140 – Margat was held from the Princes of Antioch by the Mansoer family, who sold it to the Knights Hospitallers in 1186. The order must almost immediately have embarked on a massive programme to strengthen the defences. By 1188 these were already formidable enough to deter Saladin, who passed Margat by on the devastating raid that drove the Crusaders from so much of the jebel. As a result Margat became even more vital to the Franks. By 1203 the reconstruction of the castle was substantially complete. Margat defied sieges in 1204 and in 1280, by when the Crusaders' critical shortage of manpower was only too apparent, but was taken in 1285 by the Mameluke Sultan Baibars after a siege of over five weeks.

Two roads climb steeply to the castle, one up the northern flank of the hill, the other, reached from a marked turning off the northbound motorway, circling from the south-west. Whichever way you take, it makes sense to follow the narrow road that runs round the huge roughly triangular enceinte, and then to motor on uphill – trying to avoid the attention of the soldiers guarding the summit – to look down on the massive defences intended to protect the vulnerable southern angle of the site.

The castle is entered through the West Gate, which is reached by a bridge over the dry moat constructed under the Arabs. It is worth pausing to survey the outer wall, the section of which on the left is strengthened by rounded towers. A vaulted vestibule opens to the narrow court between the inner and outer walls. After some 30 metres/100 feet the inner barbican gate of 1270 is on the left. Resist the urge to continue downwards between the walls and enter the gate, which opens to a handsome vaulted space. Cross this, if time does not press, to enter the large area enclosed by the outer fortification, much of which is littered with rubble from later residential structures. The walls overlooking the valley to the east are reasonably well preserved, and it is instructive to see how well the inner fortress was defended even from this side.

Return to the barbican and leave it by a door in the south wall. Beyond this a door opens to the undercroft of what must have been a particularly handsome chamber, possibly the chapterhouse, with vaults rising from leaf capitals. Ahead is the central courtyard, irregular in plan. Opposite is the chapel, to the left of which are two massive magazines or storerooms. That nearer the chapel is backed by an even larger such space, linking with the formidable round east tower. Work has recently been done on the terraces above the magazines.

The chapel, built soon after the Knights secured Margat, is a masterpiece of architectural discipline and restraint, beautifully exemplifying the muscular response of the Crusaders to the subtleties of the early Gothic taste of metropolitan France. Decoration is minimal. The outer portals on the west front and to the north were enriched with mouldings and with small columns – only those of the lateral door survive – and the columns between the two bays of the interior bear capitals inspired by the Corinthian order. The chapel is not large, yet seems unexpectedly spacious. The altar was set in the raised apse, small doors from which lead to two rooms contrived within the angles of the structure. In one of these are the remains of murals, with apostles in the Byzantine tradition.

No other such scheme survives from the Crusader kingdom.

Stairs on the north side of the building give access to the roof, from which one can continue to that of the adjacent block, with large halls on two floors, to the south, and then to that of the great donjon. An internal stair in the north wall of this leads down and one can cross to the upper hall, from which one can look down into the chapel. The donjon, which the Hospitallers had probably built by 1203 and is rounded on its exposed sides, is a formidable structure. The ultimate line of defence, this towered over the exposed salient at the snout of the site, which was protected by the outer wall, and by the considerable ditch intended to cut the fortress off from the rising ground beyond. The Hospitallers were right to concentrate their efforts here. But ultimately these were to prove unavailing. The south tower of the outer wall, which echoed the donjon in design, was successfully undermined by Sultan Qalaun's engineers, and its fate more or less settled that of the castle. The Mamelukes took care to reconstruct the tower after their victory.

To the west of the donjon is the most ambitious secular interior of Margat, the vaulted great hall. This overlies a substantial cistern. The southern end of the building has fallen. From here the sightseer can choose to return to the central court, or follow stairs in the donjon that lead out to the space between the inner and the outer walls. It is worth following this round to the left, to examine the formidable outer walls of the donjon, the adjacent block and the chapel. You can then retrace your steps and follow the path between the walls back to the barbican gate. In whatever order Margat is explored, one is left with an enhanced respect for the unremitting sense of purpose of the Hospitallers.

Margat.

51. QALAAT AL-KAHF

The Crusaders and the Ayyubids were both masters of the art of military architecture. Their masonry at its best is incomparable. The Assassins, less refined as builders, were, however, fully their equals in their exploitation of the mountainous terrain of their territories in Iran and in Syria. Qalaat al-Kahf perfectly exemplifies this. This evocative fastness on a massive cliff-walled rock above the junction of three plunging valleys lies at the heart of the Jebel Ansariye, hidden by high ranges from almost every line of approach. No Syrian castle vies with al-Kahf in the untrammelled grandeur of its setting, hemmed in by the luxuriant greens of the vertiginous ranges that guard it: the only recent intrusion is the asphalt approach road.

This may take some persistence to find. In the town of Sheikh Badr turn left for Ain Breisin, and there, after some 4 kilometres, turn right and after 3.9 kilometres right again, to cross a dam over a deep valley. Go left after 1.7 kilometres, to turn right 0.2 kilometres further on, then left at 0.9 kilometres and left again after 1.2: the road climbs upwards and then descends, to end after some 4 kilometres just below the east face of the rock.

The potential of the site was recognized in the late eleventh century by the Banu Munqidh, who held Shaizar from 1081 and may have constructed their castle in about 1120. This was sold to the Ismaelis, known to the Crusaders as the Assassins, perhaps in 1138, and was no doubt remodelled by them. From 1164 Qalaat al-Kahf served as one of the main bases of Rashid al-Din Sinan, the 'Old Man of the Mountain', who died there in 1193. It was here that Count Henri of Champagne, Regent of the Kingdom of Jerusalem, came in 1197 to appeal for the support of the Ismaelis against his Sunni adversaries. Sinan's successor astonished his guests by instructing two of his adherents, no doubt heavily drugged, to throw themselves from the cliff.

As the Crusader state shrank, the Ismaelis were increasingly exposed to the attentions of the Mamelukes. Qalaat al-Kahf fell to Sultan Baibars in 1273. This remained in occupation, as, for example, an inscription of 1388 near the gatehouse attests. What survived was evidently damaged in 1816 as a result of a punitive expedition of the governor of Tripoli, who had – as she believed – been prevailed upon by the irrepressible Lady Hester Stanhope to rescue a kidnapped French captain.

The outcrop crowned by the castle runs from east to west, sloping gently in the latter direction. A path runs up below the cliff on the north side, reaching the first gate, the fallen lintel of which bears an elegant Kufic inscription. Higher up is the main gate, cut through a protrusion of the cliff which is thought to have given the castle its Arab name, meaning 'castle of the cave'. Just outside this is a shallow niche surmounted by an arch, and an inscription carved into the cliff. There is also an inscription inside the gate. Just beyond this a path on the right leads to the ruinous hammam, in the centre of which there is a bath chamber with a central octagonal pool. Evidence of rather sophisticated plumbing can be seen. An inscription records that the bath complex was built in 1176.

Beyond the gateway the path mounts the recently excavated ramp, with two flights of rock-cut steps, some of which were grooved to prevent slipping. The ramp leads to a further gate, marked by the longest inscription on the site. A potential enemy then had to negotiate three ninety-degree turns, before reaching another rock-cut ramp and negotiating a final turn to the left through the inner gate. To the west, in effect an outer bailey defended by vestigial walls above the cliffs, is a level area with a number of cisterns, now much overgrown. There was a round tower at the western extremity. Further east, where the ridge narrows, the walls were more massive. Traces of buildings can be identified, and the footings of others, cut from the rock, have been revealed by the archaeologists. The inhabitants clearly paid much attention to water catchment.

But it is not only for the ruins that one returns. Whether in the spring sun or in driving rain, the castle has an irresistible appeal. The views are unimpaired, and it is only too easy to imagine the two hapless Ismaelis launching themselves into the abyss *pour épater* the Franks. Then there are the flowers – cyclamen, pale pink and white, in the crevices and small purple orchids; and even in the wind the air is laden with the heady scent of the fiercely yellow broom.

The approach to the castle.

52. TARTUS: TORTOSA

Tartus is a dusty enough place, and the austere cathedral apart, the remains of the Crusader city have been subsumed in the living town, itself now overshadowed by the hotel blocks on the corniche and industrial development to the north. But what survives more than justifies the time that must be taken to unravel the more promising of the threads.

Originally a dependency of Phoenician Arwad, known as Antaradus, the town had a Christian community at an early date and became a centre of the cult of the Virgin, celebrated for a picture of her that was held to be by St Luke. With such credentials it is hardly surprising that the place became a city under the Emperor Constantine, in whose honour it was renamed Constantia in 346 by his heir. Taken by the Arabs but recovered in 968 by the Byzantines, only to fall to the Fatimids in 997, Tartus was controlled by Tripoli at the time of the First Crusade. Held briefly by the Franks in 1099, Tortosa, as they termed it, was retaken by Raymond of Toulouse in 1101 to become the key northern fortress of his county of Tripoli. The scale of the cathedral begun in 1123 implies the importance that the Marian cult they revived at Tortosa had for the Crusaders. Although attention was also paid to the defences of the city, this fell to Nur al-Din in 1152. It was quickly recovered, and made over by the King of Jerusalem to the Knights Templar. Their subsequent work on the defences was not able to prevent Saladin from sacking the city in July 1188. He did not have time to invest the donjon and marched on in search of easier prey. The shock evidently stimulated further work on the defences, which resisted Sultan Baibars in 1267 and again in 1270. Tortosa only fell to the Mamelukes, after all the inland

The cathedral: west front.

castles that had previously protected it had been lost, in 1291.

The Crusaders' Tortosa was laid out as a rectangle, narrowing as the lie of the ground dictated from north to south, with its west side to the sea and the inner citadel fanning out from the north-western corner, the donjon at the centre of its sea wall. The scale of the city is most easily understood from the waterfront, now a wide asphalt motorway, tamed only when wind whips the spring tides over the low embankment. A tower, now overwhelmed by its concrete neighbours, marks the south-western corner of the city. Some 400 metres/quarter of a mile to the north is the southern tower of the citadel. Much of the seaward wall of this survives, some 350 metres/yards in length. From the north-west corner, the northern wall of the citadel wall is relatively easily followed. After 200 metres/218 yards, this turns south, protected by the inner moat. The lower city wall, however, continues for a further 200 metres/218 yards beside a modern road, and then turns south and disappears.

The outer wall of the citadel is most easily studied on the east side, where a stretch of the moat survives. The wall was partly built on rock-cut footings; and, particularly in the lower sections, much of the original Crusader masonry survives, with fine blocks, many of which are bossed. Later housing has encroached: downpipes rust and render decays; washing dries in the wind; and an old man searches among the long grass. The tower in the centre of the outer northern wall stands to first-floor level, a noble vaulted chamber now put to service as a mosque. The inner walls were even more formidable, defended by numerous turrets and backed by a series of barrel-vaulted storerooms.

In the centre of the citadel there is an irregular open space. To the west is the donjon, only the lower section of which survives, much encroached upon by housing. Parts of the original glacis are in place. The spectacular large vaulted hall, now used as a restaurant, is entered from a postern on the seaward side of the wall. On the north side of the court is the impressive mass of the Great Hall, built against the curtain wall. Stairways and passages between the houses make it possible to inspect the extant upper windows and fragments of the vault at close quarters. The chapel is to the south-east of the hall. This was of four bays, of which the first two are choked with houses. The simplicity of Templar architecture is beautifully demonstrated in the way the pilasters dividing the bays run up into the vault, much of which is intact.

The most remarkable building of Tortosa is unquestionably the cathedral. The position of this in the centre of the Crusader city was clearly determined by that of the Byzantine shrine it replaced. Construction began in 1123, but was still unfinished at the time of Saladin's raid, which evidently took a heavy toll. When the Templars resumed work they were aware that the structure might need to be defended and added towers at the eastern corners. The austere west front was built during this phase. The solidity of this is beautifully emphasized by the elegance of the lancet windows, which are framed by colonnettes that support their finely moulded projecting hoods. The sides of the cathedral are given relief by the buttresses, which help to bear the massive weight of the ceiling.

The interior of the cathedral, with a nave flanked by narrower aisles, must always have come as a surprise after the brilliant Syrian sunlight. If possible, ask the custodian to turn off the electric light, for the power of the architecture is much clearer when natural light filters through the narrow windows and gives relief to the great cruciform piers that flank the nave. Perhaps because this replaced the earlier structure, the central apse is not symmetrical. It was here that St Luke's likeness of the Virgin was housed. The cathedral was conceived in the last phase of the Romanesque, but by the time it was completed the style we now term Gothic was already firmly rooted in France. If the slightly pointed arches of the interior hint at this revolution in taste, the fenestration of the west front confirms its progress. Such details as the leaf capitals are equally eloquent.

When the Templars left they took the picture of the Virgin. The cathedral

was left to decay. The French, with characteristic atavistic zeal, restored it in an exemplary fashion. It now serves as the archaeological museum. The exhibits are inevitably outshone by their setting, but nonetheless of interest. Finds from Amrit include a statuette of a man sheathed in a folded robe. There are seven later Phoenician sarcophagi with formulaic heads, the closed lips and open eyes of which are oddly disconcerting. A large Roman sarcophagus takes the place of the high altar, and a mural of the Circumcision evokes the Byzantine past.

The fortress: eastern bay of the chapel.

53. ARWAD

The island of Arwad, an oval some 0.8 kilometres/half a mile in length by no more than 300 metres/ 328 yards in width and 2.5 kilometres/1½ miles from Tartus, had an historic importance out of all proportion to its size. From the shore it seems to float on the water's surface. There are regular boats from the little harbour at Tartus. In 1992 a quick glance at their rusting metalwork would have put me off going, if Edouard de Pazzis, who had travelled with me from Aleppo, had showed the slightest weakening of his sangfroid. He didn't. But I must admit that it was almost a relief when I last tried to go, only to find that there were no sailings because of heavy seas.

The Canaanites were the first people to recognize the potential of the island, which has the twin advantages of a dependable fresh-water spring and the best natural harbour between the Orontes and Tripoli. Mentioned as an entrepôt in texts of late in the second millennium BC from Amarna, Arwad was subsequently conquered by the Pharoah Tuthmosis III. With Tyre it became one of the major centres of the Phoenicians, dominating their other settlements in the area. The island fell in turn to the Assyrians and the Persians, but its king had the sense to submit to Alexander the Great in 333 BC, and the place thus preserved a degree of independence under the Seleucids. This was lost with the arrival of the Romans. Arwad was the last outpost of Byzantine Syria to hold out against the Arabs, falling in 640, and the Templars' fortress on the island held out for eleven years after the loss of Tartus, until 1302.

The port is in the north-eastern section of the island and thus protected to some extent from the prevailing wind. The Phoenicians threw out a

The Phoenician wall.

pier, part of which survives as the spit of land cutting into the harbour. But the most visible of their works is the great sea wall. Stretches of this, with fine Cyclopean blocks that have withstood the tides of two and a half millennia, survive to the west and south-west of the island. The centre of this is now densely inhabited and largely built over. A small fragment of the Crusader fortress survives near the heart of the town, while a minor Arab fort near the harbour has become a museum. Arwad is very much of a tourist resort for the Syrians. But despite the summer crowds, there is something strangely moving about the place. And it is not perhaps altogether fanciful to imagine that the blood of the Phoenicians still courses in the veins of the boat builders of Arwad, who seem to express an instinctive artistry in their traditional carpentry.

54. AMRIT

The scattered remains at Amrit are among the most curious in Syria, and, in Burns's words, reflect 'the ability of the Phoenicians to absorb and syncretize outside influences'. The rather modest tell was first settled late in the third millennium BC, perhaps by colonists from Arwad. The compound of the temple of Melqart attests to the importance the place had assumed late in the sixth century, as the Achaemenid Empire extended its rule to the eastern Mediterranean. The temple was still in use when Alexander swept through Syria in 330 BC and made Marathos, as the town was then known, his base while Damascus was secured. He will no doubt have thought the name auspicious, and the form of the temple would have fascinated a man who recognized the importance of respecting the cults of others. The rise of Tartus heralded the eclipse of Amrit.

It is easy enough to get to the slumbering ruins. A turn to the right off the Tripoli road, some 3 kilometres/2 miles from the southern end of Tartus, heads for the north side of the site, which has happily been spared from development. After crossing a stream, the Nahr al-Amrit, a lane leads to a small car park, and continues to pass the Temple of Melqart, the Phoenician counterpart of Hercules. This owed its existence to the spring that rose below the tell and was thought to have medicinal qualities. The water was fed to a rectangular pool, which was flanked except on the northern side by a colonnade, the rear walls of which were cut from the rock and now provide a congenial habitat for numerous cyclamen. The columns are square, as is so often the case in Egypt; the parapet above these was originally decorated with merlons, the triangular projections so characteristic of Iranian architecture of the time. The northern ends of the east and west colonnades were marked by towers,

of which little now survives. In the centre of the pool, on a rock-cut base, is the sanctuary itself, with a cornice of Egyptian type which was crowned by merlons, some of which have been restored. Despite unnecessary floodlighting, the temple is strangely moving at dusk, when the croaking of hundreds of frogs makes it seem almost alive.

The tell is to the east of the temple. Beyond this, where the lane ends, is the unexpectedly impressive amphitheatre, partly cut from the rock, presumably of Hellenistic date. A rupestrian house lies to the south-east of the tell. Some 700 metres/half a mile south of the latter are two cylindrical towers, presumed to be of the fourth century BC. On the base of one are four lions, all unfinished. Burial chambers are associated with both monuments, and there is much evidence of surface quarrying in the area. A kilometre/two-thirds of a mile further to the south is the Burj al-Bezzaq, or 'Tower of the Snail', another mausoleum, built of massive blocks and originally surmounted by a pyramid. Beyond, and of interest only to the persistent, is what survives of an obelisk. It is revealing that the builders of Amrit experimented with such characteristically Egyptian forms, for, like Arwad, Amrit was in close economic touch with the ports of Egypt; and the Egyptian deity of medicine, Echmoun, came to be associated with the temple complex, which evidently attracted pilgrims from a wide area.

Amrit, alas, has suffered since its monuments were recorded in the early nineteenth century for Sir Robert Ainslie by his travelling draftsman, Luigi Mayer. But there is much to see amid the open pasture and the pinewoods.

The temple, from the north-east.

55. QALAAT YAHMUR AND SAFITA:

Chastel Rouge and Chastel Blanc

The Crusaders could never take control of the Syrian littoral for granted. And we are fortunate that so much evidence survives of their defensive system in the hinterland of Tortosa.

About 10 kilometres/6 miles south-east of Tartus on the road to Safita turn right at Beit Shalluf on a narrower road, which after 2 kilometres/just over 1 mile reaches the central square of the village of Yahmur. To the north-east stands the best preserved of the lesser Crusader forts in Syria, on the site of an earlier Byzantine strongpost. The original Crusader castle, which no doubt subsumed the earlier structure, was in turn reconstructed after Chastel Rouge was made over to the Knights Hospitaller in 1177. The place was taken during Saladin's campaign in 1188. Quickly recovered, it was held by the Crusaders until 1289, when it was seized for Sultan Baibars as he closed in upon Tortosa, which was to surrender two years later.

The castle consists of an oblong donjon, set within a rectangular outer wall, with a gatehouse on the south and projecting angle-towers at the north-west and the south-east corners, which may have been added by the Mamelukes. Storerooms and stables were built against the outer walls and stairs mount to the corner towers. The lower floor of the keep is a smaller variant of its far grander counterpart at Saone, with a vaulted ceiling supported on a central pier. On my first visit, early one morning in 1995, a youth showed me with some pride pin-ups of a favoured Dutch footballer which he had attached to the pier, quite undisturbed by the fact that his mother was still in bed near by. Younger children watched as I moved carefully in the gloom – for the narrow arrow slits were the only source of light – not wishing to damage the household goods, or indeed

Qalaat Yahmur, from the centre of the modern village.

Safita: the donjon.

the inevitable television. When I left, the boy dismissed the tip I proferred with a patrician disdain. Yahmur has now been sanitized: the family and their animals have gone, and the castle has been tactfully restored.

The upper hall of the donjon, similar to that below, is entered from the terrace on the west. And stairs lead up to the roof, from where the defenders could see not only Tortosa but two of the castles further inland which protected it: the Templars' Arima, now as rewarding for its rural context perhaps as for what survives of the Crusaders' time, and the great donjon of Chastel Blanc some 20 kilometres/12½ miles away.

To reach this, return to the main road and continue. For much of the journey the donjon is in view, crowning the ridge upon which the substantial town of Safita has grown up in its shadow. Chastel Blanc, so named from the colour of its limestone before this weathered, was in 1112 held by the Count of Tripoli, Bertrand of Toulouse. Nur al-Din tore down the original Crusader castle in 1167. The Templars, already responsible for Tortosa, took over, but further damage was caused by an earthquake in 1170, and by the opportunistic Nur al-Din a year later. The Templars restored the donjon, but it had to be substantially reconstructed after a second earthquake in 1202. That this survives in remarkably good order is in part due to the pusillanimous decision of the Master of the Templars to evacuate the castle in February 1271 rather than face the formidable army of Sultan Baibars, which was approaching on its way to assault the Hospitallers' stronghold of Krak.

The town of Safita has an unexpected charm, partly because of the many stone houses on the narrow roads that follow the steep contours of the hill. Long an Alouite preserve, the town came in the late nineteenth century to be predominantly inhabited by members of the Greek Orthodox Church, who are now, however, no more than a small minority. Much of the outer wall survived until late in the Ottoman period, but virtually all of this has disappeared.

As you enter the town it is easy to work out how to reach the donjon.

This is best approached from the east. A road climbs steeply up to the site of the former gatehouse. Within this, at first-floor level, was a most handsome chamber of which the rear wall and two of the supports of the vault are in place.

The donjon is an admirably uncompromising building, 18 metres/60 feet in width and some 27 metres/90 feet high. For there was nothing frivolous about the Templars' view of defensive architecture. The small door, which seems almost to have been punched into the west façade, opens to the austere, and unexpectedly spacious, chapel of the order, now the Greek Orthodox parish church of St Michael. Apart from the door, the only sources of natural light are five narrow windows. If possible, encourage the sacristan to turn off the electricity, to see how subtly the architecture works. The side walls are divided into three sections by pilasters, which bear the vaults, 18 metres/60 feet high. The bowed apse is flanked by a pair of sacristies. A steep flight of stairs in the south-eastern corner rises to the wonderful vaulted space on the upper floor, which was used by the Knights. This is divided into two sections by three cruciform piers, the weight of which is borne by the vault of the chapel below. Light filters through the arrow slits. The staircase continues to the roof, which is protected by arrow holes and battlements. This remains an extraordinary vantage point. The garrison of Chastel Blanc was in signalling range of Tortosa and Krak, of Arima and Chastel Rouge, and in a position to monitor hostile movements in a wide swathe of territory. As the sounds of the modern town rise, it is sobering to remember that muscular and disciplined as the donjon of Castel Blanc is, this and its counterparts ultimately proved in the language of today not to be fit for purpose, because the whole Crusader endeavour was ultimately unsustainable.

56. HUSN SULEIMAN

Husn Suleiman, the ancient Baetocaece, is incontestably the most atmospheric of the major classical sites of Syria. It cannot of course compete in grandeur with the Temple of Bel at Palmyra, or in scale with the temenos wall of Damascus. But it is unmatched in the way the huge complex lies within a fold of a high terraced valley, hidden from below in the wilds of the Jebel Ansariye.

The earliest shrine was a Canaanite or Semitic high place. This was subsumed in a Phoenician sanctuary dedicated to a local manifestation of Baal, the god of Phoenician Arwad. It became a major place of pilgrimage. After Arwad was drawn into the orbit of Alexander and his Seleucid successors, the cult of Baal gradually came to be assimilated with that of Zeus; one of the Seleucids granted Baetocaece to Zeus, giving the sanctuary freedom from some taxes and instituting bimonthly fairs that would continue to be held for half a millennium. The cult of Zeus Baetocaecian continued to flourish after the Roman takeover. The extant sanctuary, begun in the first century AD, was substantially built in the late second century. Apparently never finished, the complex was abandoned on the official adoption of Christianity in the fourth century, although later a church was put up near by.

Husn Suleiman is surprisingly difficult to find, although it can be reached from Safita and from Bait al-Rafieh on the main road between Masyaf and Krak des Chevaliers: from Safita take the road due north, marked for Dreikish, but fork right on the fringe of the town, continuing to the north-east for some 20 kilometres/12½ miles, before turning left for Ain ash Shams, which is beyond the ruins.

Pause to survey the sanctuary from above. This adheres to the traditional Syrian plan, found at Damascus and Palmya and Baalbec, as

well as on a more intimate scale at Amrit, with a relatively small temple set in a very much larger rectangular walled compound, here aligned from north to south. There is a scattering of modern houses, one alas almost too visible on the higher ground to the south. A tethered donkey brays as one approaches the ceremonial propylaeum in the centre of the north wall. With porticoes on either side, this was richly decorated, with a finely carved lintel protected by the relieving arch above, subsidiary doors and elegant niches. The delicacy of these elements is enhanced by the massive simplicity of the flanking walls, built of Cyclopean blocks – some as much as 10 metres/33 feet long – and adorned at the corners by lions. An inscription of about 255 on the propylaeum states that the co-Emperors Valerian and Gallienus confirmed the ancient grants made to the sanctuary by the Seleucids.

From the gate one is aware of the scale of the temenos, which is 85 metres/278 feet wide and about 134 metres/440 feet deep. Where worshippers once gathered a woman is desperately trying to round up her five cows. Ahead, beyond a free-standing altar for gifts, is the temple, originally of pseudo-peripteral form, with an Ionic portico and matching pilasters round the cella walls, much of which survive. A stair within the wall presumably originally led to the roof. Among the fallen debris is a fine lion mask.

There are fine subsidiary gates near the centres of the lateral walls, and a third in the south wall behind the cella. Like that of the propylaeum, the lintels were all carved on their lower sides with eagles, associated with Zeus, and the stars of morning and evening, Phosphorus and Hesperus: that of the east gate is reasonably well preserved. The lintels of the lateral gates are supported by winged victories. The east gate bears an inscription of 171 recording that the monument was paid for by local subscription. I lingered as clouds blew by and the rain came and went, moved by the

The west gate.

conviction of those who mobilized Cyclopean blocks with such effort and surprised to find that pale blue hyacinths had found a habitat between the fallen stones.

A second and smaller temenos lies across the road to the north-west of the sanctuary. There is a small and elegant temple, with an Ionic portico in antis and an eagle above the door. Behind this are vestiges of a church of basilica type and the ruin of what may have been a nymphaeum. Farm traffic passes, but nobody seeks to disturb the sightseer, who may feel a strange reluctance to leave a haunting place that nestles in the protection of the hills and must seem cool even when the summer heat beats down upon the Phoenician coast.

57. KRAK DES CHEVALIERS

Krak des Chevaliers is the *ne plus ultra* of the medieval castle. Nothing, not the Emperor Frederick II's Castel del Monte, still less any of the Welsh fortresses of King Edward I, can stand in comparison. For T.S.R. Boase, whose beautiful book on the Crusader castles I was given on two successive Christmases by a godfather who understood my tastes, the Krak ranked with the Parthenon and Chartres, and was the 'supreme example' of a medieval castle. Like others I went first to Krak des Chevaliers with almost impossible expectations, in no way diminished by a distant sighting from Chastel Blanc. I drove up through the township of al-Husn with a sense of mounting excitement. This has never been dispelled. Commanding an incredible, but alas now scarred, panorama, whether louring under dark cloud or in rain, or brilliant in sharp sunlight that reveals the precision of the Crusader masonry, the Krak is a mesmerizing building. It can disappoint only those who like ancient monuments to be ruinous.

The castle crowns a promontory of the Jebel Kalakh and commands from the north the vital Homs Gap, the Buqeia, squeezed between the Lebanon range and the Jebel Ansariye, that links Homs and thus the desert to the east with the coast. The site was first fortified in 1031 by a strategically astute Emir of Homs. During the First Crusade Raymond of Toulouse briefly occupied the place. But it was recovered by the then Emir, only to fall in 1110 to Tancred, the subtle, even brilliant, yet unscrupulous and at times disloyal Regent of Antioch, who, as Sir Steven Runciman wrote, 'grew wiser as he grew older'.

The Krak became part of the county of Tripoli, held by descendants of Raymond of Toulouse. Because of the prohibitive expense of protecting the exposed Crusader frontier, Raymond II of Tripoli made over the

The castle, from the south-west, with the aqueduct.

castle to the Knights Hospitaller in 1144. A major building campaign was undertaken in the following decades, and the walls of the inner fortress are of this period. Nur al-Din was defeated below the Krak in 1163. The Knights embarked on a further programme of reconstruction after 1170, a year in which the area was hit by a serious earthquake. In 1188 it took Saladin only a day to realize that the castle could not be taken quickly and decide to march on in pursuit of easier prey. The outer walls were largely completed by the early thirteenth century, and further improvements were made in a third campaign after 1250, by when the Crusaders' position was increasingly under threat. But despite an evident shortage of manpower, the Krak continued to receive tribute from Homs' rival Hama until 1267.

From then the garrison was more or less cut off from the hinterland by the Mamelukes. The formidable Sultan Baibars laid siege on 21 February 1271. On 31 March the outer wall was breached, apparently by the north-western tower above the aqueduct. Without hope of a relieving force, the defenders had no sensible alternative but to surrender. They did so on 7 April, and were allowed to go to Tripoli on condition that they return to Europe. While the Crusaders retained their last outposts in Outremer, and there was even the hint of a threat from Cyprus, the castle was worth maintaining. The Mamelukes made good the damage they had caused and were responsible for a number of significant modifications, principally to the outer towers to the south, east and north. But with time the fortress as such was abandoned. Later a village grew up within the walls. In 1934 the last inhabitants were moved as part of a major but exemplary programme undertaken by the French, who regarded the place as a 'monument de France', in much the same way that the Italians in their restoration of Leptis and Sabratha thought to bolster their 'historic' claim to rule Libya.

The entrance is on the east, through a tower which dates from the last phase of Crusader construction – and is notably smaller than the two Mameluke towers to the left. The door, faced in metal, is also apparently of Mameluke date and an elegant inscription records Baibars' recommissioning of his prize. Within the walls, a vaulted ramp rises to the left, passing a long guard room. After some 130 metres/142 yards the ramp doubles back to the right, to turn though a gate in the inner wall of the castle, which was originally defended by further doors and by a portcullis. This opens to the irregular Lower Court.

Opposite is the delicate loggia that fronts the Great Hall, and on the right the austere chapel, flanked by the stair to the Upper Court. The loggia of seven bays is in the purest French Gothic taste. Some of the stone has had perforce to be replaced, but such details as the ball-leaf capitals are of an exquisite refinement. Burns translates the text on the right-hand window as: 'Grace, wisdom and beauty you may all enjoy but beware pride which alone can tarnish the rest.' This is oddly apposite, for as the Hospitallers passed though the two doors to their Great

Hall they little thought that this beautiful statement of the most modish French architectural fashion would within less than a generation be lost to them.

The large twelfth-century Great Hall is very different in character. The vaulted ceiling rises from capitals decorated with leaves of ivy, oak, vine and other plants. But these apart the builders aspired to an uncompromising solemnity. Behind the hall is a vast covered space within the inner walls, which served for utilitarian purposes, with storerooms, kitchens – near the southern end an oven for bread survives – and lavatories. From the south end of the hall can be reached a yet vaster and more tenebrous covered area, used for warehouses and as barracks. Silence now prevails in the gloom.

The thirteenth-century bastion below the south-east tower, with lion statues.
Right **The glacis.**

The chapel, one of the Hospitallers' earlier projects, is admirably austere. The simple vaulting rests on restrained pilasters, to which the spectator's sense of space is partly due. The restraint of the building meant that this lent itself to conversion as a mosque in 1271.

The narrow stairway which partly blocks the main doorway of the chapel may have been built during the siege of that year. The Upper Court is an excellent viewpoint. The Tower of the King's Daughter is part of the twelfth-century scheme, but the upper section is Mameluke. The tearoom within this is not always open.

Descend to the Lower Court and then mount the broad flight of steps by the entrance gate to the south terrace, leading to the three great southern towers that constituted the donjon of the Krak. The largest is on the left, at the south-eastern angle of the inner circuit. Both this and the central tower, the Tower of Monfret, are rectangular in plan but rounded at the exposed southern ends. The two towers are not parallel but were set at an angle to each other and originally linked by a platform. The third tower, at the south-west corner, is round and noticeably less massive. A spiral stair leads to a beautiful circular room, with airy vaults rising from small columns, a row of rosettes and a beautiful window with embrasures. Here, no doubt, lived the Master of the Hospitallers or his representative. Even in metropolitan France it would be hard to match the elegance of the room in any secular interior of the date, about 1260. The stair continues to the roof, which is for Burns the 'best vantage point' of the castle. There are views to Safita and even to the coast, marred alas by the unworthy intrusion of new buildings on the rising ground to the south-west. The tower is linked to the Monfret tower by an external terrace, defensive in purpose, with a vertiginous prospect of the great glacis that protects the southern flank of the inner fortress.

To examine the outer walls return to the gate to the Lower Court and, at the top of the ramp, follow a passage on the left that leads to the area between the two enceintes. By the outer northern bastion there is a barbican, now closed. Beyond is the first of the five bowed towers of the outer western wall, named after the windmill this once bore. More rewarding is the remarkable Tower of the King's Daughter. This breaks forward dramatically from the curve of the inner wall. High up is a row of blind arches, three of which masked openings from which to bombard any enemy attacking the wall below. Later, when the tower was heightened, a second row of arches was added for the same purpose. The glacis of the west face of the inner wall is impressive. Near the centre, this is interrupted by a circular bastion, from which a gallery was reached. Further on, at the south-western corner, is the round tower of the donjon. The outer wall is equally well preserved. And it is worth following at least in part the passage that links the towers and climbing to the upper walkway.

From the south-western angle, one is mesmerized by the astonishing glacis that rises so inexorably from the reservoir and is fused so seamlessly with the towers of the donjon above. Nothing in medieval military architecture quite matches it. It is difficult to tear oneself away to survey the outer defences to the south. These centre on a substantial square tower, probably begun by the Crusaders but reconstructed in 1285 for Sultan Qalaun, as an inscription establishes. The round towers that flank this were built under Baibars, that to the north probably replacing a predecessor destroyed in the siege of 1271. Just to the south of this is the elegant aqueduct that brought water from the higher ground to the west. Beyond the reservoir is the bastion added by the Hospitallers after 1250 to protect the entrance ramp. This is, rather unexpectedly, decorated with two lions. A passage between the bastion and the southern tower of the donjon leads to the sharp bend in the entrance ramp.

Anyone who visits the Krak will wish to survey it from outside. There are wonderful views from the road that follows the outer walls and then turns towards the unfortunate new tourist facility, which so mars the view from the castle. Equally spectacular is the more distant prospect from the as yet untrammelled valley to the north, which leads to the flourishing Monastery of St George.

GLOSSARY

Absidal Of an apse.

Acropolis Fortress of a city or town.

Agora Square or marketplace.

Ambulatory Colonnaded extension to a temple or church.

Apodyterium Dressing room of a Roman bath.

Bab Gate (Arabic).

Basilica Type of Roman hall with lower side halls, which was used for many Byzantine churches.

Bema Raised area in chancel of a Byzantine church.

Caldarium Hot room of a Roman bath.

Cardo maximus Main colonnaded street of a Roman town, usually running from north to south.

Cella Central chamber of a temple.

Decumanus Main cross street of a Roman town, usually running east to west.

Deir Monastery (Arabic).

Donjon Keep of a castle.

Exedra Semi-circular recess.

Fane Temple.

Forum Marketplace.

Frigidarium Cold room of a Roman bath.

Glacis Sloping area, rock cut or built, below a defensive wall.

Hammam Bath (Arabic).

Hippodamian grid Type of town plan on a grid with segments, devised by Hippodamus of Miletus.

Hypogeum Underground tomb chamber.

Iwan Arched space opening off a courtyard (Arabic).

Jebel Mountain (Arabic).

Kalybe Open-fronted shrine.

Keep Inner stronghold of a castle.

Khan Caravanserai, or warehouse-cum-hostel.

Madrasa Koran school.

Maristan Institution for the sick, in body or mind.

Mimbar Pulpit with steps to the right of a mirhab (Arabic).

Minaret Tower of a mosque.

Mirhab Niche in mosque, aligned on Mecca (Arabic).

Muqarnas Decoration with stalactite-like triangular forms, used in niches and domes (Arabic).

Narthex Vestibule at west end of a church.

Necropolis Cemetery.

Nouria Waterwheel (Arabic).

Nymphaeum Fountain building.

Odeon Small theatre-like building used for meetings.

Orchestra Semi-circular space between the stage and auditorium of a theatre.

Orthostat One of a series of stone slabs lining a wall of a major building.

Peribolos Sacred enclosure.

Peristyle Covered colonnaded corridor round an internal courtyard, or outer colonnade of the cella of a peripteral temple.

Pilaster Engaged column.

Praetorium Residence of a Roman governor, or barracks.

Principia Roman military headquarters.

Propylaeum Monumental entrance to a temenos.

Qalaat Castle (Arabic).

Qasr Palace (Arabic).

Stela, stelae Upright stone slab(s), generally inscribed.

Strata Diocletiana Road from Sura on the Euphrates to Damascus.

Suq, souk Market (Arabic).

Tell Mound built up by the debris of long-term occupation.

Temenos Sacred enclosure.

Tepidarium Warm room of a Roman bath.

Tetraporticus Portico of four columns.

Tetrapylon Four-sided structure at the intersection of major roads in a Roman city.

Transept Lateral extension of a church.

Turba, turbe Tomb, tombs.

PEOPLES AND DYNASTIES

Abbasids Rulers of Damascus from 750 to 968.

Achaemenids Rulers of the Persian Empire, who secured Syria as a result of Cyrus the Great's conquest of Babylon in 539 BC, and held it until the defeat of Darius by Alexander in 333 BC.

Akkadians Rulers of the empire founded by Sargon (c.2340–2150 BC).

Amorites People who founded kingdoms in northern Syria of the Early Bronze Age.

Aramaeans People who settled in Syria after 1200 BC and founded the Neo-Hittite cities in northern Syria in the ninth century.

Assassins Ismaelis, from Iran, who built up a power base in the Jebel Ansariye in the twelfth century but were suppressed by Sultan Baibars in 1270–3.

Assyrians Mesopotamian state that dominated Syria from 856 to 612 BC.

Ayyubids Dynasty founded by Saladin, which controlled Syria from 1176 until 1260.

Banu Munquids Family which held Shaizar from 1081, of which the best-known member was the autobiographer Usamah Ibn Munqidh.

Byzantines Successors to the empire transferred in 330 from Rome to Byzantium, later renamed Constantinople, which controlled Syria until 636, and recovered territory in northern Syria in 969, finally losing this in 997.

Crusaders Christians who sought to recover the Holy Places and defend these, occupying much of the coast of Syria in 1198–9 during the First Crusade and losing their last outpost in Syria, Arwad, in 1302.

Druzes Adherents of a religious sect founded by the Fatimid Al-Hakim (996–1021), long settled in the Lebanon, many of whom migrated to the Hauran in the nineteenth century.

Fatimids Rulers of Cairo who controlled Syria in 969–1055.

Franks Crusaders.

Ghassanids Christian Arab tribe allied with the Byzantines in the sixth century.

Hellenistic Phase of Greek rule in Syria that began with Alexander's victory at Issus in 333 BC and endured until the collapse of Seleucid power after 164 BC.

Ismaelis Sect inspired by the eighth-century Ismael, son of the sixth Imam; see Assassins.

Macedonians Subjects of Alexander the Great, many of whom remained in the service of his successor in Syria, Seleucus I Nicator.

Mamelukes A military oligarchy that held power in Cairo and controlled Syria from 1260 until the Ottoman conquest of 1516.

Maronites Adherents of a Christian sect, concentrated in the Lebanese mountains.

Mongols Central Asian tribes united by Genghis Khan, whose successors invaded parts of Syria in devastating waves between 1260 and 1401.

Nabateans Arabs whose control of trade routes to the south allowed them to build up a substantial position in southern Syria, from which they were driven by the Romans in the first century AD.

Neo-Hittites See Aramaeans.

Ottomans Turkish dynasty, with capitals successively at Bursa, Edirne and from 1453 Istanbul, which added Syria to its empire in 1516, was at its zenith under Suleiman the Magnificent (1520–66) and held Syria until 1918.

Palmyrenes Semitic people of Palmyra, who controlled much of the trade from east to west from the first century BC and unsuccessfully challenged Rome in 267–72 and in 273.

Parthians Rulers of Persia until AD 224.

Phoenicians Semitic peoples based in coastal cities in Syria and the Lebanon who in the second millennium BC developed extensive commercial links with other states, later founding a network of colonies throughout the Mediterranean world, maintaining a degree of independence at Arwad and elsewhere until the Roman era.

Sasanians Rulers of Persia from 224 AD, who in turn challenged Roman and Byzantine control of Syria.

Seleucids Dynasty founded by Seleucus I Nicator (311–281 BC), which ruled Syria from Antioch.

Seljuk Rulers of empire built by descendants of Seljuk, notably Alp Arslan, who defeated the Emperor Romanus at Manzikert (Turkey) in 1171.

Semites An early people whose descendants settled in Syria from the Early Bronze Age, at Mari, Ebla, Aleppo and elsewhere.

Sumerians Early Bronze Age civilization in Mesopotamia.

Umayyads Dynasty of Caliphs established by Moawiya (661–81) at Damascus.

CHRONOLOGY

BC

c.3300–2250	Early Bronze Age.
c.2250–1550	Middle Bronze Age.
c.1550–1200	Late Bronze Age.
c.1200–539	Iron Age.
c.900–800	Neo-Hittite states. Assyrian domination.
539–333	Persian control.
333	Defeat at Issus of Darius II by Alexander the Great (336–323).
301	Occupation of Syria by Seleucus I Nicator (311–281).
198	Conquest of southern Syria by Antiochus III (223–187).
64	Annexation of Syria by Pompey.

AD

105	Annexation of the Nabatean kingdom by Trajan (98–117).
187	Marriage of Septimius Severus (193–211) to Julia Domna, daughter of the High Priest of Emesa.
244	Foundation of Shahba by Philip the Arab (244–9).
272	Defeat of Zenobia at Palmyra by Aurelian (270–5).
306–37	Reign of Constantine.
451	Condemnation of Monophysites at Council of Chalcedon.
458	Death of Simeon Stylites.

573	Syria raided by Chosroes I.
621–4	Conquest of Syria by Chosroes II.
636	Muslim victory over the Byzantines at the Battle of the Yarmuk.
661–750	Umayyad Period.
661–81	Caliphate of Moawiya.
750–968	Abbasid Period.
754–75	Caliphate of al-Mansur.
969–1055	Fatimid Period.
1055–1128	Seljuk Period.
1071	Seljuk victory over the Byzantines at the Battle of Manzikert.
1097–1102	The First Crusade.
1098	The conquest of Antioch by the Crusaders.
1118	Al-Ghazi invited to Aleppo.
1128–74	Zengid Period.
1176–1260	Ayyubid Period.
1176–93	Reign of Saladin.
1187–92	The Third Crusade.
1260	Invasion of Syria by Mongols under Hulaga.
1261	Defeat of the Mongols by the Mamelukes at Ain Julad.
1266–1516	Mameluke Period.
1291	Fall of Tartus to Sultan Qalaun.
1300–3	Fourth Mongol invasion.
1516	Ottoman conquest of Syria.
1918	Entry of the Allies to Damascus.

1918–19	Reign of Feisal.
1920	France granted the Mandate of Syria and of the Lebanon.
1925–7	Revolt that began in the Hauran.
1939	Antioch and the Hatay ceded to Turkey by France.
1946	Syrian independence.
1958–61	Syria united with Egypt to form the United Arab Republic.
1970	Premiership and, from 1971, presidency of Hafiz al-Assad.

INDEX

Page numbers in *italic* refer to illustrations

C

D

E

F

G

H

I

J

K

L

M